"This much is clear—Jesus turns the wc
includes human morality. RW Glenn m
Crucifying Morality: The Gospel of the l

—R. Albert Mohler, Jr.,
President of Southern Baptist Theological Seminary

"The first thing to recommend is that you meet RW Glenn in person. God's
sanctifying work in this Jersey boy is extraordinary, at least to us Minneso-
tans. But if you can't just up and meet RW yourself, second best is taking
up this book. Here you'll get a taste of this singularly interesting person,
but much more importantly, you'll find fresh glimpses of his Savior and
Sanctifier. Jesus himself likely will come alive for you in the Beatitudes like
never before."

—**David Mathis**, Executive Editor, Desiring God

"I love to laugh and I love to study theology. These two enjoyments don't
often intersect, which explains why I'm such a fan of RW Glenn's Drive
By Theology podcast. In *Crucifying Morality*, RW brings along his grand
sense of humor and his ability to make theology clear for the average Christian. He clears away the fog of confusion from the Beatitudes which are
widely misunderstood and misapplied. The Sermon on the Mount is all
about Jesus—who knew? If you want to experience the joy and freedom
that issue from a gospel-centered Sermon on the Mount, this book was
written for you."

—**CJ Mahaney**, Sovereign Grace Ministries

"There are two maladies that have plagued Christians for centuries, the
disease of self-righteousness and the illness of insecurity. God does not
want his children to suffer with either. Instead, he wants us to walk in joy
and victory. But how do we consistently walk the razor thin line of the
gospel with neither pride nor uncertainty? Dive into this book. RW Glenn
is one of the most insightful, helpful and careful theologians of our day.
Let him help you find the joy of your Savior once more."

—**Todd Friel**, host of Wretched TV & Radio

"This may come as a surprise to you, but morality can be dangerous. Or,
more specifically, our pursuit of morality can be dangerous. Without a
proper grounding in the "It-Is-Finishedness" of the gospel, the quest to
become moral can simply turn into just one more self-salvation project.
In this short book, my friend Bob Glenn shows how, in the Sermon on the
Mount, Jesus demolishes all notions that we can reach the righteousness
required by God and thereby exterminates all attempts at self-sufficient moral
endeavor. Bob articulates well that our hope is not ultimately anchored in
our becoming like Jesus. Rather, our hope is ultimately anchored in the fact
that Jesus became like us."

—**Tullian Tchividjian**, Pastor of Coral Ridge Presbyterian Church
author of *Jesus + Nothing = Everything*

"Finally, a handling of the Beatitudes that doesn't leave me depressed and cynical, a complete loser who's been given a moral "to do" list I have no chance of keeping, knowing I'll be hammered if I don't. Glenn left me hopeful and motivated because he helped me see that the Beatitudes aren't a moral code for me to achieve, rather a beautiful portrait of Jesus who achieved it all on my behalf. They're not eight steps to becoming righteous in God's eyes, but rather eight powerful arguments for why your only hope is Jesus. Read and let yourself weep. Read and let let loose and celebrate."

—**Paul Tripp**, Paul Tripp Ministries, author of *Broken-Down House*

"Bob Glenn has a booming voice that needs to be heard. I rejoice in the way this book leverages the Sermon on the Mount to show us our spiritual poverty and Christ's all-sufficient glory. Full conformity to the Sermon on the Mount is essential to our salvation; and thankfully Jesus Christ did exactly that. And now by beholding the One who lived the Beatitudes and inherited their blessings, we can find ourselves being transformed into his likeness. *Crucifying Morality* does an excellent job of expositing the Beatitudes, while focusing our gaze upon the only Person who perfectly lived its precepts."

—**Milton Vincent**, Pastor-teacher at Cornerstone Fellowship Bible Church in Riverside, CA., author of *A Gospel Primer for Christians*

"*Crucifying Morality* is a powerful reminder that the Christian life is not primarily about what we do, but who we are in Christ. Bob Glenn has given us a terrific overview of what life in the kingdom looks like by leading us to encounter the world-shattering truth of the Beatitudes."

—**Trevin Wax**, Managing Editor of The Gospel Project, author of *Holy Subversion and Counterfeit Gospels*

"Bob Glenn helped me to see how I want to grow: with my eyes on Jesus, resting in him and his righteousness, growing in these beatitudes, and looking forward to even more. Like a great novel, I couldn't stop turning the pages because each one was clear and encouraging, and the next seemed to be more so."

—**Dr. Ed Welch**—Senior faculty member CCEF, author of *Shame Interrupted*

"How we interpret Jesus' words in the relatively few lines of the Beatitudes reveals our approach to the Christian life to be either primarily moralistic or gospel-istic. If you see the gospel in the Beatitudes, then you really see it. Glenn sees it clearly and in his fresh voice helps us to see it in every area of life, every aspect of faith, every difficult situation, every single Beatitude."

—**Rick James**, Publisher CruPress, author of *A Million Ways To Die*

"Jesus is the Beatitudes. That's the heart-winning message of RW Glenn's *Crucifying Morality*. We are tempted to think that the focus of the Beatitudes is our performance, but the message of *Crucifying Morality* is that Jesus is the Beatitudes . . . for us! He fulfilled them for us so that we can forever enjoy the incomparable blessedness of his life! That's the good news of *Crucifying Morality*! Get this book, read it, and don't keep its message to yourself."

—**Dan Cruver**, President of Together for Adoption

CRUCIFYING
MORALITY

THE GOSPEL OF THE BEATITUDES

RW GLENN

Shepherd Press
Wapwallopen, Pennsylvania

© 2013 by Robert W. Glenn
Trade Paperback ISBN: 9781936908530

eBook ISBN
Mobi format: ISBN 9781936908486
ePub format: ISBN 9781936908493

Published by Shepherd Press
P.O. Box 24
Wapwallopen, Pennsylvania 18660

Unless otherwise indicated, all Scripture quotations are taken from The Holy Bible, English Standard Version. Copyright ©2001 by Crossway Bibles, a division of Good News Publishers. Used by permission. All rights reserved. Italics or bold text within Scripture quotations indicate emphasis added by author.

Page design and typesetting by Lakeside Design Plus
Cover design by Tobias' Outerwear for Books

First Printing, 2013
Printed in the United States of America

VP 22 21 20 19 18 17 16 15 14 13
14 13 12 11 10 9 8 7 6 5 4 3 2 1

Library of Congress Cataloging-in-Publication Data:

Glenn, R.W., 1971-
Crucifying morality : the gospel of the Beatitudes / R W Glenn.
   pages cm
ISBN 978-1-936908-53-0 (trade pbk. :alk. paper) --ISBN 978-1-936908-48-6
(Mobi) -- ISBN 978-1-936908-49-3 (epub ebook) 1. Beatitudes--Criticism, interpretation, etc.
2. Bible. N.T. Mathew V, 3-12--Criticism, interpretation, etc. I. Title.
BT382.G53 2013
241.5'3--dc23
                            2013004118

eBook: *Crucifying Morality*
Go to http://www.shepherdpress.com/ebooks

To Joseph M. Babij

pastor, mentor, friend

TABLE OF CONTENTS

PREFACE

HOW TO USE THIS BOOK

The deacons of my church have forbidden me from using a chainsaw. Not because there was some horrible, disfiguring accident, but because my reputation for not being handy is legendary. It once took me six hours to change a light fixture in my family room. That thirty-minute job became nearly an all-day adventure because—and this is crucial—because I got cocky. I tried to change the fixture without reading the directions. So, as much as it's true that I'm not naturally very handy, I do a lot better if I read the manual first. As long as I follow the directions, I'm in pretty good shape.

So think about this preface as a manual for the book you are holding in your hands. This "how to" should help you get the most out of it.

First, you will notice footnotes as you go through the chapters, and though this book isn't reserved for scholarly types, you may want to further your study by following those footnotes to other teachers and writers who have much more to say on the Beatitudes than this book will cover.

Second, at the end of each chapter, you will find discussion questions designed to help you think through what you have read—either by yourself or, even better, with a group of fellow readers. Each chapter features four sets of questions:

- "For Your Head" provides general comprehension questions to point you back to key concepts in the chapter.
- "For Your Heart" suggests questions that probe your interior life and invite you to think about how the teaching of the chapter changes you personally.
- The section of questions called "For Your Church" asks you to connect what you learned in the chapter to your local body of believers, making application to corporate spiritual growth and ministry.
- "For Your City" presents questions that move beyond what you might think of as your "spiritual" circles to your neighbor who may or may not go to church and to your general neighborhood or town or region, asking you to make connections between what you learned in the chapter and what you experience in your larger community.

As you read this book, you may learn something new about the Beatitudes, or you may reconsider what you thought you knew about the introduction to the Sermon on the Mount. Either way, I hope you will use the tools you discover here to enhance your understanding of the Beatitudes and deepen your thrill in the gospel.

1

JESUS CRUCIFIES MORALITY AS YOU KNOW IT

Blessed are the cheese makers.

— *Monty Python's Life of Brian*

Blessed are the poor . . . the peacemakers . . .
the persecuted.

— Matthew 5:1–12

I have never been thrilled about flannelgraph. Maybe you remember those paper cutout characters from Bible stories that your Sunday school teacher, Mrs. Anderson, put up on a felt board as she told you about Noah and the ark, David and Goliath, and Jonah and the whale (I know—it's really a "big fish"). Ring any bells? Flannelgraph?

Maybe you are too young to remember it, but you don't have to in order to understand my problem: flannelgraph was guilty of the sin of omission. I never saw the flannelgraphs for Noah getting naked and drunk in Genesis 9, Onan wasting his "seed" in Genesis 38, or the Levite and his ravished and then dismembered concubine from Judges 19. I am not saying that these stories *ought* to be included in the visual aids section of a children's Sunday school curriculum, but this kind of "sugar and spice and everything nice" approach to the Bible neuters the word of God, giving the wrong impression about the Christian faith and the nature of the gospel.

Something analogous has happened to Jesus' Sermon on the Mount, especially the Beatitudes, and not just as it appears in children's Sunday school classes, though I vaguely remember the flannelgraph for that one: Jesus' hair was the same as mine in 1983, parted in the middle and feathered back. He was holding, I think, a lamb or a round-faced cherub of a child on his lap while the teacher retold the sermon in the most mellifluent tones imaginable:

> "Jesus said, 'Blessed are the poor in spirit, for theirs is the kingdom of heaven.' Children, what does it mean to be poor in spirit?"
> "It means to be totally dependent on God," we recited in unison.
> "Good. Now be good little boys and girls and be totally dependent on God."
> "Yes, Mrs. Anderson."

Do this to children and they will be indoctrinated into a false view of arguably the most radical introduction to a sermon ever given. This kind of teaching reinforces the nearly irresistible tendency we all have to reduce Christianity to a system of works-righteousness because it turns a list of declarations regarding the nature of a child of the kingdom into a list of dos and don'ts.

A Radical Introduction

Of course, you may think exactly that about the Beatitudes. Maybe it is a passage of Scripture that you have heard since childhood, just like I have. You were taught then that the Beatitudes were the highest form of morality that anyone could live by, and you know now how impossible they are. Or maybe you never experienced the flannelgraph version of the Beatitudes. Nevertheless, they still seem complicated to you, and you don't see people around you acting like they are a big deal. Certainly, few others think Jesus is serious here because no one can take this stuff literally.

So maybe it is time to get unfamiliar. Maybe you need to read these verses with fresh eyes for the first time. Whatever your exposure to the Beatitudes has been, you probably think of them as less powerful and captivating and helpful than they are. Take a step back to see how breathtakingly radical their real message is.

We begin with the problematic first word: "blessed." If you compiled all of the pages ever written on that one concept within the Beatitudes, you would have a much bigger book than this one. The word is hard to translate directly, and we have difficultly understanding the idea. Here is a quick survey of what others have said about it:

- Strong's Concordance translates the word that Jesus uses here as supremely blessed, fortunate, well-off, and happy.
- Martyn Lloyd-Jones called the blessed man one "who is to be congratulated . . . envied, for he alone is truly happy."[1]
- D. A. Carson suggests that to be blessed means to have God's approval.[2]
- John MacArthur calls this concept, "'blissful,' not a superficial feeling of well-being based on circumstance, but a deep supernatural experience of contentedness based on the fact that one's life is right with God."[3]
- Ed Welch says that "the blessed are honored, their status is enviable, they are obvious recipients of divine approval and favor. Replace 'Blessed are' with 'How honorable are' and you will see what I mean."[4]
- Phillip Yancey suggests that "lucky"[5] is the closest we get to this concept in contemporary culture simply because it is the kind of happiness you cannot deserve or earn or work up on your own.

Being *blessed* by God is not something that you earn or achieve. God gives blessedness as a gift: he shows favor to people who have no right to it whatsoever. It is simply an expression of God's grace, which is always a surprise. Indeed, as Yancey said, our culture understands this concept as luck, and that makes sense, because if you are a Christian, God has blessed you through no doing of your own. You are the privileged recipient of his divine favor. You are the fortunate one.

Do you know that kind of happiness? Can you even begin to imagine what that feels like? Even if you can, you certainly would not call "blessed" the kinds of situations Jesus names in these verses. Try these culturally updated translations of the Beatitudes on for size:

- Blessed are the poor in spirit. = The destitute are actually loaded with excessive riches.
- Blessed are those who mourn. = Congratulations! You have deep sadness!
- Blessed are the meek. = What a privilege to be obscure!
- Blessed are those who hunger and thirst for righteousness. = The losers win all the time.
- Blessed are the merciful. = Got a bleeding heart consumed with meeting the needs of others? You've got it going on.
- Blessed are the pure in heart. = The religious fanatics have God's approval.
- Blessed are the peacemakers. = Sissies are the best.
- Blessed are the persecuted. = The persecuted have such great luck!

We might call these the Bizarro Beatitudes because they seem so illogical and antithetical to our contemporary mindset. Can you imagine your coworker running up to you to congratulate you for being persecuted? "Hey, congratulations on having your face kicked in for Jesus. Way to go!" Would you think of this as sincere congratulations? Of course not! You would probably think that it is *because* of guys like him that you've had your face rearranged. If you could rewrite the Beatitudes to reflect what you really think about being blessed by God, what would they say?

- Blessed are the self-sufficient and self-reliant and independent.
- Blessed are those who have fun, enjoyable, pain-free lives.
- Blessed are those who have made a name for themselves.
- Blessed are those who have the best résumés.

- Blessed are those who reward hard work, oppose laziness, and judge people only by their merits.
- Blessed are those who are only mildly committed to their religion.
- Blessed are those who mind their own business.
- Blessed are those whom everyone likes.

That sounds like the anti-gospel. Nowhere does the Bible support these kinds of claims. Suddenly, the Bizarro Beatitudes seem more on target than we might like to think. Jesus says you are to be congratulated—sincerely congratulated—if you are the object of people's scorn, ridicule, and violence, because you know that God's blessing is on you. That may take a while to sink in, but that's the radical reality of the Beatitudes.

No wonder the flannelgraph and the saccharine tone of those reductionist Sunday school lessons can't get the job done. Jesus' teaching is too radical to be stuck on felt. He uses counterintuitive gospel logic to show us that life in the kingdom of God is completely contrary to what we expect. In fact, we could not have predicted it. Kingdom blessing looks like the opposite of everything we value. So don't moralize the Beatitudes, sterilizing the gospel as though it is primarily or even only a rulebook for nicer living. You cannot put the mind-altering, world-shattering nature of the Beatitudes into neat categories. Jesus won't let you.

A Beautiful Introduction

Even as the Beatitudes rock your world, pause to contemplate how beautiful they are. The more you reflect on them, the more you want them—the more you admire them. Just think about the kind of person they describe. And think about what kind of person you would rather have as a friend. Someone blissfully oblivious to life in this broken world or someone who weeps for the oppressed? Someone who knows she's nice or someone who admits her flaws? Someone with a zero-tolerance policy for people with self-inflicted messy lives or someone who sacrifices to help you clean up yours?

And what do you find more admirable? Gratifying your every desire or resisting some desires for causes that are bigger than you? Defending yourself when you're right or compromising in order to preserve the relationship? Being liked by everyone or suffering for doing what's right?

As counterintuitive as the Beatitudes are, there is something simultaneously winsome about them. There is a deep, gospel logic here that reveals itself the more you contemplate what Jesus actually says. Maybe it really is blessed to be poor in spirit, mournful and meek, starving for righteousness, merciful and pure in heart, a peacemaker, and a persecuted minority. Jesus makes you think. He makes you stop and take stock of the sum total of your life. Who am I? What is life all about? What am I living for and longing for? What's truly important to me? The Beatitudes are meant to jar you from your complacency and lead you to question whether you have entered the kingdom.

Dos and Don'ts

If you grew up in the church, you may have heard a teacher say something like: "What's a beatitude? It's Jesus saying, 'Be At This Attitude.'" He would then go on to claim that in the Beatitudes, Jesus is saying, "If you want the kingdom, *be* poor in spirit, mourn, *be* meek, hunger and thirst for righteousness, *be* merciful, *be* pure in heart, *be* a peacemaker, and *be* persecuted." It may have come across as though you had better achieve the qualities celebrated in the Beatitudes or you were out of luck.

But nothing could be farther from the truth. It is no accident that the Beatitudes contain no imperatives whatsoever. Because we are wired for performance and have an insatiable hunger to turn Christianity into a system of dos and don'ts to *earn* a spot at the table of grace, we feel almost irresistibly inclined to turn them into commandments. Instead, they are the qualities that begin to characterize sinners who encounter God's grace in the gospel.

Don't get me wrong. I am not against commandments. There are very clear demands of the gospel—imperatives that Christians are expected to obey. In fact, as the Sermon on the Mount continues, Jesus gives sixty-six commands. So my problem is not with commandments per se but with reading texts that *are not commandments* as though they are. Do we really want to go beyond what is written and *add* to the Sermon on the Mount? Of course not. No Christian in his right mind thinks he can or should add to the teaching of the Lord Jesus Christ.

So what are we to do with the Beatitudes? What *does* Jesus mean here?

Think of the Beatitudes as a gospel litmus test. They show you how much (or how little) your faith is in the gospel of grace. The context for the whole Sermon on the Mount is, after all, Jesus preaching the gospel (see Matthew 4:23). In the Sermon on the Mount, Jesus simply teases out the implications of believing the good news of his life, death, burial, and resurrection. Thus, in the introduction to that sermon, Jesus describes the kind of character who must wrestle with those implications.

In the Beatitudes, it is as if Jesus says, "If you want to know that you have come to believe the gospel I have been preaching, look for these qualities in your life." Then he goes on to describe what people who possess those qualities will do in the world. The Beatitudes presuppose that you have turned from your sin and self-righteousness to trust in Jesus as the one who lived the life you could never live and died the death you deserved to die and now gives you the benefit of that life and death as a free gift. If you stand on the sure foundation of that grace, *then* you can live like a child of the kingdom—then you can understand and obey the sixty-six commands that follow the Beatitudes.

Christians, because they have come to understand the grace of God, *are* people who are poor in spirit, who mourn and are meek, who hunger and thirst for a righteousness not their own, who exude mercy and purity of heart, who make peace, and who experience persecution for Jesus' sake. The Beatitudes are a profile of the Christian. They are a description of people who would never dream of turning the characteristics God has given them by grace into a list of moral commands because they know that Jesus has crucified even their best attempts at self-centered, self-propelled morality on the cross. The grace of Jesus is all they have: they know they cannot muster up on their own the characteristics Jesus calls blessed.

This is why every approach to the Beatitudes that turns them into commandments to keep, mandates to fulfill, or imperatives to obey turns them into something contrary to what Jesus intended. The Beatitudes declare what a child of the kingdom looks like; they do not list dos and don'ts that get you in the kingdom.

Jesus Christ Is the Beatitudes

Therefore, do not seek poverty of spirit. Seek Jesus. As you see what it cost the heavenly Father to save you, you will see yourself as bankrupt beyond words. Seek Jesus, and you will mourn not because of what your sin cost you, but because of what it cost your heavenly Father. Seek Jesus, and meekness will overflow in your life. Who can take a posture of superiority at the foot of the cross?

Seek Jesus, and you will find all the righteousness you will ever need: his perfect record given to you freely as a gift. Seek Jesus, and you will be merciful, for the most needy recipient of a handout is the person you see in the mirror every day. Seek Jesus, and you will find your heart more and more singular in its devotion to God and more willing to be honest with other people. Seek Jesus, and you will continually sheath your sword and seek reconciliation with others because you know the utter serenity achieved between you and God by the blood of Jesus. Seek Jesus, and you will gladly bear reproach for his name.

Do not seek the Beatitudes. Do not turn them into moralistic teaching. Seek Jesus Christ who alone embodies the Beatitudes, and the Beatitudes will *then* be true of you as well. Why? Because Jesus fulfills them:

- Jesus is the most spirit-poor and meek person ever to have lived, "gentle and lowly in heart" (Matthew 11:29).
- Jesus mourned more thoroughly for your sin than you do, "very sorrowful, even to death" (Matthew 26:38) as he considered God's wrath against it.

- Jesus lived a perfectly righteous life, truly acceptable to God, such that even unbelievers like Pilate's wife recognized it (Matthew 27:19).
- Jesus has all mercy and responds to requests for mercy with miraculous healings (Matthew 20:29–34).
- Jesus has a completely pure heart of devotion to his Father: "Not as I will, but as you will" (Matthew 26:39).
- Jesus makes ultimate peace, bringing sinners into the most holy place through his reconciling death (Matthew 27:51).
- Jesus is the persecuted one *par excellence*: unjustly condemned, mocked, scourged, brutally beaten, and crucified, yet triumphant because he entrusted himself completely to his Father (Matthew 27:26; 28:6).

The Beatitudes are all about Jesus. Seek him through the gospel and you will be a new person, enjoying all the benefits of a relationship with God, living in the kingdom. Christianity is about coming over and over again to rest in the life that Jesus lived and the death that he died for you as a gift of sheer grace. Religion and morality turn Christianity into a system of achievement: "Do this, and you will live." But the Beatitudes turn this on its head. In them we hear Jesus say, "I have done this, *so* you live." And when you hear his voice ringing out clearly in the language of the Beatitudes, you will discover more and more just how blessed you are.

FOR YOUR HEAD

1. What does the word "blessed" mean?
2. What is wrong with reducing the Beatitudes to moralistic teachings or commands?

FOR YOUR HEART

3. What was your first exposure to the Beatitudes? Before reading this chapter, what would you have said they were about?
4. Did you resonate more with the Bizarro Beatitudes or with the "culturally acceptable" list that followed them? How closely do your values align with the world around you?

FOR YOUR CHURCH

5. Does your church take the Beatitudes seriously? How or how not?

6. How would you introduce the Beatitudes to a children's Sunday school class?

FOR YOUR CITY

7. What are the most prized qualities in your particular circles? Think about what people talk about: education, physical attractiveness, social clubs, car brands. What idols do the people in your city seem to favor especially?

8. Where does Jesus' kind of blessedness rate in your city? Do people around you prize the kind of happiness he seems to mean here? How and how not?

2

THE GOOD NEWS
OF MORAL BANKRUPTCY

Learning to love yourself: it is the greatest love of all.
> – Michael Masser and Linda Creed,
> "The Greatest Love of All"

Blessed are the poor in spirit, for theirs is the kingdom of heaven.
> – Matthew 5:3

Popular culture often portrays heaven as a fine alternative to hell (if you believe in that kind of thing), but also as the most dreadfully boring place in the universe. Everyone who dies and goes to heaven lands in a benign version of the Department of Motor Vehicles: you sit around in a kind of waiting room as disembodied spirits play harps and float on clouds while you wait to get into a place that makes The History Channel seem scintillating. But it's better than the DMV, because instead of all of the attendants being mean and cranky and overworked, everyone's sweet enough to give you a toothache.

21

And who's there with you? Everyone who was mostly good by earthly standards. Men who helped old ladies cross the street even though they had just cheated on their wives. Women who regularly served in soup kitchens but who maxed out credit cards to fill their closets with clothes they never wore. People who mainly did no harm, or at least did enough good to balance it out. Merely moral people who are inclined to find heaven boring because it doesn't specialize in all the cool stuff they had on earth and hoped to find inside the pearly gates.

When Jesus tells us that the poor in spirit get the blessing of heaven, he runs counter to our cultural picture of heaven and provides the antidote to mere morality. Trying to live well enough to squeak into heaven simply will not prepare you to enjoy the kind of eternity Jesus has prepared.

The Kingdom of Heaven

The Bible describes heaven as the place where everything becomes more real, more vivid, and more vibrant than on earth. If you are a Christian when you die, then your soul departs to be with Jesus, who is the sum total of all that is good, true, and beautiful (Philippians 1:23). What could be better than to enjoy him in his very presence? But the time between your death and the return of Jesus to earth is not all there is to heaven. Instead, when Jesus returns he will resurrect your body, reunite your body with your soul, and restore the heavens and earth to an even more glorious condition than before we fell into sin (Revelation 21). We look forward to "life *after* life after death."[6] Heaven is getting to live the fullest life imaginable in a perfect world with Jesus Christ forever.

But Jesus means more than that when he mentions heaven in this beatitude. The Jews of his day would have understood the word *heaven* as a circumlocution for *God*—a way of saying *God* without actually saying *God*, which would have been construed to violate the third commandment (Exodus 20:7). They did everything they could to avoid saying the divine name, like substituting words associated with God (words like *heaven*) for *God*. So when Jesus talks about the kingdom of heaven, he certainly does not mean some otherworldly disembodied kingdom, nor specifically the place where Christians go when they die or even life after life after death. The kingdom of heaven simply refers to the kingdom of God.

What exactly does Jesus mean by the word *kingdom*? Most basically, the term *kingdom* refers to something dynamic, not something static like a geographic or political or spatial realm; instead, the kingdom is the regime, rule, or reign of God. It is God's powerful reign as king of the cosmos, being exercised right now over absolutely everything. As I write these words, the Lord is micromanaging every last detail of the universe, down to its tiniest particle: "The LORD has established his throne in the heavens, and his kingdom rules over all" (Psalm 103:19).

Here, however, Jesus means a more specific subset of God's sovereign rule over everything.[7] This kingdom fulfills a promise that God made his people concerning a day when he would save them from all their enemies and exercise his power such that everything that had gone wrong with the universe because of our rebellion in the garden of Eden would be set straight. In Isaiah 11:1–7, God describes his kingdom as a place that enjoys complete wisdom, understanding, strength, fear of the Lord, justice, righteousness, faithfulness, and peace. Indeed, in the kingdom of heaven, every aspect of salvation is fully realized.

Our Broken Kingdom

When we consider the state of our existence as a result of the fall, the idea of God's kingdom coming to earth sounds appealing. After all, when we rebelled against God's authority in the garden and decided to run our own lives apart from his rule, everything about our existence was poisoned. Our physical bodies now become infirm (subject to sickness, disease, defect, and death), and the entire creation suffers similarly. Nature no longer performs for us as it should, so blights and famines cause deprivation and starvation. But nature doesn't just make things difficult for us; it brings disaster into our lives through killer storms and tornadoes and earthquakes.

Our relationships were also poisoned in such a way that people with wealth and power can oppress the weak and the poor and even *cause* poverty for others. People without wealth can envy to the point of theft or even kidnapping and murder to get what they want. Relationships are messy now—marriages, families, and friendships all suffer from the fall. We commit all kinds of transgressions against one another.

And what about how we view ourselves? A war rages in our hearts with all kinds of competing desires—desires for good, but also for evil, supported by an irresistible inclination to do what God forbids. We lie to ourselves about our value, thinking too highly or too lowly of ourselves rather than simply seeing ourselves as God's image-bearers. We often live our lives thinking that God made us as empty cups to be filled up with affirmation, approval, and acceptance, rather than as conduits for God's glory. In addition, we can be overcome with grief, mourning, tears, and the often excruciating pain of emotional wounds.

Closer to the core, our very ability to discern good from evil was poisoned. As a result, we became particularly susceptible to the schemes of the destroyer. Some toxins in the earth cannot be explained by human evil but only by supernatural forces of evil. Spiritual forces seek to destroy us and keep the virus of our own rebellion in our bloodstream. There is a real devil who uses his evil power to leverage our sins against us.

But the source of all our trouble is that our hearts are now poisoned against our God. We are at odds with him, and he is at odds with us. My heart wants to have its own way, and it cannot stand to have God in charge of my life; it desperately wants to disobey him while taking some credit for all the good things he has given me, including my own niceness or religiosity. Left to my own devices, I kick and scrape to preserve my own little kingdom of Bob—even though it is thoroughly broken, and I am thoroughly contaminated.

The Kingdom of God

The world is a messed up place and we are messed up people in it. We are assailed by physical problems and psychological problems and interpersonal problems and theological problems. We also suffer from additional trials caused by supernatural agents of evil. And it is at this point precisely that the kingdom of heaven comes in. Just at the right time! God promised that a time would come when he would usher in his reign of comprehensive rescue. That is the kingdom of heaven that Jesus spoke about. And it is the power of that kingdom that Jesus' ministry manifests throughout Matthew's gospel. For example,

- The kingdom of heaven is present when Jesus heals the sick: "And he went throughout all Galilee, teaching in their synagogues and proclaiming the gospel of the kingdom and healing every disease and every affliction among the people" (Matthew 4:23).
- The kingdom of heaven is present when Jesus casts out demons and ultimately defeats Satan and all the forces of supernatural evil in the universe: "And if I cast out demons by Beelzebul, by whom do your sons cast them out? Therefore they will be your judges. But if it is by the Spirit of God that I cast out demons, then the kingdom of God has come upon you" (Matthew 12:27–28).
- The kingdom of heaven is present when Jesus feeds the hungry (Matthew 14:13–21, 15:32–38).
- The kingdom of heaven is present when Jesus subdues nature, like when he calms a storm with a word and walks on water (Matthew 8:23–27, 14:22–33).
- The kingdom of heaven is present when Jesus performs miracles that confirm him as the king who ushers in the rule of God: "Go and tell John what you hear and see: the blind receive their sight and the lame walk, lepers are cleansed and the deaf hear, and the dead are raised up, and the poor have good news preached to them" (Matthew 11:4–5).

- The kingdom is present when Jesus reconciles sinners to a restored relationship with God (see Matthew 22 but also the entire scope of Matthew's gospel).

The kingdom is present in Jesus' person and ministry, but this does not mean that everything has *already* been set right. Just pick up the newspaper and you will see that things are still not right in the world. Only when Jesus comes back will the kingdom he inaugurated be consummated. The kingdom of heaven is a present reality (an "already" experience), but it is also a future hope (a "not yet" event). For example, in Matthew 26:29, Jesus says to his disciples, "I tell you I will not drink again of this fruit of the vine until that day when I drink it new with you in my Father's kingdom." But here in the first beatitude, Jesus emphasizes the manifestation of the kingdom in the present: "Blessed are the poor in spirit for theirs *is* the kingdom of heaven." The poor in spirit get to enjoy in the here and now the future and final renewal of all things, even as they await the day when all things will be made completely new.

A Heavenly Kingdom Without a Heavenly King

Who would not want to live in a kingdom like that? Wouldn't you want the effects of sin in your life to be reversed? Of course, you would. We all would. But there is one small problem. We want the *blessings* of the kingdom of heaven, but we do not want heaven's *king*. Like the people in a story Jesus told, we say, "We do not want this man to reign over us" (Luke 19:14). We do not want to bow the knee to the king of God's blessed kingdom. We prefer to think that we can find some respite from the evils that we face and still retain a little self-rule.

We look to the kingdoms of man—to governments who will protect us and provide for us and make us prosperous. Even the best earthly governments experience corruption, while others are bold-faced, cruel, and oppressive dictatorial regimes, but we frequently fix our hopes on them. God often rebuked Israel for valuing earthly government more highly than they valued him. It seems that they did this simply because they could *see* the horses and chariots, which means they could assess their strength for themselves (Isaiah 31:1). They always remembered Egypt as a place where they ate well rather than a place where they were oppressed in slavery for hundreds of years. They did not remember God's provision. We are exactly the same.

Of course, the kingdom we flee to most often is the kingdom of self—in my case, the kingdom of Bob, complete with self-focus, self-righteousness, self-satisfaction, self-reliance, and self-glorification.[8] That is really what Israel did when they pursued help from Egypt, and it is exactly what Eve did when she ate the fruit that seemed good to her to eat. Humans have long trusted themselves and their own judgments rather than their God and his judgments. We want to rule ourselves, even if it means destruction. As John Calvin has said, "Everyone flatters himself and carries a kingdom in his breast."[9]

We look to ourselves as the king to rescue us from the evils that we face. We save ourselves from the physical effects of the fall by working out and eating right, by working hard and investing smartly. We save ourselves from the relational-interpersonal effects of the fall by looking down on others or avoiding or alienating them. We save ourselves from supernatural evil by living as if there is no devil or demons. We save ourselves from the psychological effects of the fall by denying or ignoring grief or by practicing Pollyannish optimism. We save ourselves from the problem of our alienation from God by doing everything we can to crowd out his voice. And we save ourselves from the problem of sin by justifying, rationalizing, blame shifting, lying, and covering up what we do—either by ignoring the sin or by filling our lives with enough religion or activism to somehow assuage our guilty consciences.

The bottom line is that we want to go our own way, run our own lives, fix our own problems, help ourselves. All our counterfeit kingdoms represent our common desire to rule our own world and order our own existence . . . not only apart from God but also at his expense. This is a losing proposition, for we *need* the kingdom of heaven. We need it because every other kingdom—especially the kingdom of Bob—is broken down, imperfect and impotent, just a costume kingdom, if not an evil dominion of darkness. And the only way to overcome the evils of the world and our hearts is by a change of administration: we need a new king to usher in a new reign.

Moreover, we need the kingdom of heaven to rule our hearts, not only because our alternate kingdoms and their kings are nothing but pretenders to the throne, but also because the only alternative is hell. Jesus says in Matthew 13:41–42 that "The Son of Man will send his angels, and they will gather out of his kingdom all causes of sin and all law-breakers, and throw them into the fiery furnace. In that place there will be weeping and gnashing of teeth." Even if you think you are gaining some traction in your life apart from God's kingdom, the reality is that as long as you are outside the kingdom of heaven, you face an eternity in hell.

Poverty of Spirit

Jesus has good reason, then, to say that having the kingdom of heaven is blessed. But we must remember that only a certain kind of person inherits it: the poor in spirit, or people who consciously and completely depend upon God. No longer living independently of God as the sovereign king of your universe, those with poverty of spirit live aware of their utter need for God.

We might think that to be poor in spirit means that you are shy, timid, hesitant, nervous, insecure, reserved, or cowardly. We might expect the poor in spirit to go around confessing how small and insignificant they are, like some do naturally at the Grand Canyon or on the summit of mountains. In fact, we may think some people experience such poverty naturally, as though it is a temperament or personality trait that someone could have from birth. Maybe if you just know and admit your own limitations—is that the trick to being poor in spirit? Or more than that—having some morbid notion that you are personally valueless or a piece of trash. No, poverty of spirit is not "self-hatred,"[10] self-effacement, or false humility, and you cannot work it up by your own power.

The Greek term translated "poor" here conveys a continuous state of utter poverty.[11] The poor in *spirit*, therefore, are spiritually bankrupt, morally insolvent: they have absolutely nothing to give to

God, so they rely completely on God's willingness to take care of them. This should make perfect sense because, in reality, we are all bankrupt before God. It is a simple matter of fact, just the way things are. We may try to run from it or hide it or minimize it or excuse it or blame shift it onto others, but what can we possibly take to the table of the holy God? Within our hearts, we know that "all our righteous deeds are like a polluted garment" (Isaiah 64:6). Even the best we think we can give God is filthy compared with the holiness of his being and the holiness he requires.

Our spiritual poverty is thorough, even descending beyond a zero bottom line. According to the parable of the unforgiving servant in Matthew 18, we are destitute before God *and* we owe him a debt that we can never repay because we have failed to live up to the standard we know to be right. In one sense, then, everyone is poor in spirit: we are all deeply in debt to God and incompetent to run our own lives. If you refuse to admit this, you have the shallowest kind of self-understanding imaginable, as though you were born blind but say, "I will admit that the house is dark, but not that I am not blind."[12] Such a person is simply not in touch with reality.

But when Jesus talks about the "poor in spirit" here, he does not mean people who are *objectively* bankrupt. That would be all of us. Instead, he means more specifically those who *know* they are bankrupt and acknowledge it before God, those who have a certain attitude toward the self.[13] The poor in spirit continually empty themselves of all "confidence in the flesh" (Philippians 3:4) with "full, honest, factual, conscious, and conscientious recognition *before God* of personal moral unworth."[14] Do you throw yourself so vulnerably before God and utterly depend upon him to take even one breath more?

That said, poverty of spirit cannot be the kind of earthly lowliness described above—shyness or a reserved temperament or simply knowing your own limitations or feeling insignificant or having little value or hating yourself—because it is a Godward quality, a Christ-centered characteristic. You might be a humble person by most earthly standards, but that does not mean the Lord sees you as poor in spirit; he says he looks to the one "who is humble and contrite in spirit and trembles at my word" (Isaiah 66:2). This attitude is a kind of spiritual destitution before God that you certainly cannot manufacture yourself. Even *thinking* you can simply proves that you do not understand it.[15] So poverty of spirit involves despairing of yourself, your own abilities, your own resources, and your own powers as incapable of gaining any traction with God, earning any points with the Lord, or winning any favor from Christ. The fundamental character of the Christian faith is that you live conscious of your utter dependence upon God.

Those who are "rich in spirit" cannot enjoy the kingdom of God. If you are insensitive to your own need for God to step in and take control of your life, you do not want to live where God rules. Without poverty of spirit, you can endure only one ruler: you! And you will fight to the death to preserve your sovereign rule over your kingdom of one. Only the poor in spirit want to live in God's kingdom, because they know they have nothing apart from him. They therefore sing about themselves with honest helplessness, acknowledging their desperate need for God alone:

> Nothing in my hand I bring,
> Simply to thy cross I cling;
> Naked, come to thee for dress;
> Helpless, look to thee for grace;
> Foul, I to the fountain fly;
> Wash me, Savior, or I die.
> – Augustus Toplady,
> "Rock of Ages"

You Need Poverty

You may be asking yourself, "I want to be blessed, and Jesus says I need to be poor in spirit to be blessed, so how do I do that?" But does Jesus actually tell us that we must become poor in spirit or does he simply observe how blessed the poor in spirit are? Indeed, he tells us that we must be poor in spirit without ever *commanding* us to be poor in spirit.

This might make you want to throw up your hands in despair because you cannot figure out how to be poor in spirit without doing something to get that way. Or you might think that you should sit around and just hope that somehow, someday you will wake up poor in spirit. But think about how a kingdom works. Subjects of a kingdom have work to do, and they *must* do it if they do not want to be left out (or gathered out) of the kingdom: they look to their king, they trust him, they depend on him. The only way for you to obtain poverty of spirit and therefore enjoy the blessing of the kingdom is for you to look to Christ and see what he has done for you by sheer grace through the gospel.

Think about how crazy it is to admit that you are a deeply flawed person in desperate need of divine intervention . . . unless you know the gospel of God's grace. In the kingdom of Bob, it is dangerous—no, treasonous—to confess weakness. Seeing myself as I am is scary because I will undoubtedly find problems with the ruler of my kingdom—problems that I cannot fix. In the kingdom of Bob, I trust ultimately in myself, but I know deep down that I am not reliable. A self-reliant person cannot afford to admit weakness, lest he admit that the totality of his self-reliant life is nothing more than a flimsy house of cards.

Grace, on the other hand, allows me to hear the hardest things about my flaws and patterns of sin because I know, by grace, that there is no flaw I can discover nor any sin I can unearth that can ever decimate my life. I cannot be any more loved and accepted than I am by the Lord who loves me with the full knowledge of what I have done, am doing, and will do; I have unshakable confidence that nothing can reduce his love for me. Therefore, I am free to admit my desperation. In so doing, I can experience real change, which is the very power of the kingdom of heaven in my life.

It is no accident that Jesus establishes poverty of spirit as the first and foundational quality of the Christian faith. This sets us quite clearly in God's grace, for what Jesus talks about in the Beatitudes cannot be obtained any other way than as a gift from God. You cannot earn the kingdom of God. You cannot even respond to a command to be worthy of it. Instead, you must simply consider King Jesus. For you to enter his kingdom, Jesus himself had to *die* for your sin; he had to pay the most exorbitant price imaginable to procure your admittance. You must have been poor for your salvation to cost that much. Yet Jesus *willingly* sacrificed himself for your sin, bearing in his own body the wrath you deserved—all out of love for his heavenly father and for you. Are you not humbled to the dust that he would be so willing to come after you and rescue you and make you a part of his kingdom? Watch him pay for your citizenship, and you will know poverty of spirit. There is no other way to discover poverty of spirit than at the cross.

Do you want to be poor in spirit? Meditate regularly on the truth of the gospel and you will find poverty of spirit. Look daily at Jesus: he is truly poor in spirit (Isaiah 61:1), for he became poor and died on the cross to give the riches of his poverty to you (2 Corinthians 8:9). He gave up his right to the kingdom (see Philippians 2:6) in order to bestow it on people who deserve only to wallow in the kingdoms of their own rebellion, treason, folly, and sin. Recognize your poverty, then—celebrate it, even—because it makes you eligible to receive God's kingdom by the grace of Jesus Christ. He alone can give you the kingdom you so desperately need. What marks kingdom people as genuine Christians is that they *keep coming back* to this one thing—the inexhaustible grace of God, knowing that it is all we have and all we need.

FOR YOUR HEAD

1. Explain what the kingdom of heaven is.
2. Name several effects of the fall of man. Where in the Bible, especially in the gospel according to Matthew, can you understand the tragic effects of the fall? Where can you see Jesus reversing those effects?
3. When do the poor in spirit get to enjoy the kingdom of heaven?

FOR YOUR HEART

4. We want the blessings of the kingdom of heaven but we do not want the King. Name an area in your life where you struggle to allow Jesus to reign over you.

5. How does your understanding the gospel of grace produce in you poverty of spirit? Give a specific example from the past month.

FOR YOUR CHURCH

6. What happens when you do and do not understand the gospel of grace and your own poverty of spirit in each of the following examples?
7. Someone in the church as a result of his or her own sin (addiction, lying in a business deal, or uncontrolled spending) has become financially unable to make ends meet.
8. A member of your small group sins against you by accusing you of a sin problem you do not think you have.
9. Someone from church recently experienced some kind of trial, and you gave loving counsel, lots of your time, and financial support; the person then excluded you from a social gathering.

FOR YOUR CITY

10. The culture tells us that we have all the resources within us to overcome obstacles, reconcile relationships, and be all that we can be. How would you explain this beatitude to your non-Christian friend who says that "poverty of spirit" is unhealthy?
11. How can you combat your natural tendency to be rich in spirit when you speak with your unbelieving family and friends? Can you give an example of a time when you have done this?
12. How would your poverty of spirit change the dynamics of your workplace?

3

THE GOOD NEWS OF PLEASING GRIEF AND MOURNFUL JOY

Life is pain, Highness. Anyone who says differently is
selling something.

– Westley, The Princess Bride

Blessed are those who mourn, for they shall
be comforted.

– Matthew 5:4

No one in his right mind *wants* to mourn. No one says, "I want
to experience sadness and grief as the result of really depressing
circumstances or, better yet, great suffering." On the contrary,
if we *must* experience pain, we want it to stop as soon as possible
and, in the meantime, escape by watching a movie or popping a pill
or eating a container of Häagen-Dazs ice cream. We buy into the
illusion of control, believing that if we can simply take charge of our
circumstances, all of our sadness will go away. We want to drown or
ignore or obliterate our sorrows, not celebrate them. So when Jesus

says, in essence, "Happy are the sad," he seems to be plain wrong, or else deeply insensitive.

Notice, however, that Jesus does not say mourners are blessed *because* they mourn. Rather, mourners are blessed because they shall be comforted: "Blessed are those who mourn, *for* they shall be comforted." That *for* is important, letting us know that the reason or ground for the mourners' blessedness is the certainty of comfort from God. You will be blessed not because you mourn but because you will know God's comfort.

Of course, this does not make the beatitude any less complicated. In fact, it may make it seem weirder, because now we see that in order to get God's comfort, we must first mourn. Why not skip the mourning altogether and go straight to the comfort? I will take *perpetual* comfort, thank you very much: that would be a real blessing. You would prefer a misery-*free* life to a life with misery and *then* comfort, right? Who cares if you get comfort if, in order to get it, you must experience misery first? Those who never mourn never need to be comforted—that's the beatitude we want.

The problem is that we do not understand how truly miserable we are, nor how desperately we need God to comfort us. If we did, we would mourn gladly, and then delight in God more deeply than we ever could before.

You Ought to Mourn

Only by God's grace do we see the tragedy of our sin. Those who understand the gospel of Jesus Christ hate their sin and mourn it and desperately want relief from it. But the funny thing about the gospel is that it both reveals how miserable you are and applies the specialized balm that can heal your misery. God's grace reveals how much help we need and then grants precisely that. The gospel of Jesus Christ is not good news to the comfortable, but to the uncomfortable.

Are you uncomfortable? How do you know if your discomfort is the kind that God will exchange for a beautiful wardrobe and the oil of gladness (Isaiah 61:3)? What exactly does this blessed mourning look like? We will investigate five components of those with such happy sadness: you mourn your spiritual poverty, your own sin, the sin of the world, the sin that others commit against you, and you mourn what all this sin has done to Jesus Christ.

1) *You mourn your spiritual poverty.* The poor in spirit understand their utter dependence upon God: they know that they need him because they are spiritually bankrupt, desperate for rescue but totally unable to save themselves. When you become aware of this condition, you find yourself moved to tears. Thus, the kind of mourning Jesus means here is "the emotional counterpart to poverty of spirit."[16] Mourning is the way you *feel* when you understand how spiritually poor you are. When we *sense* how spiritually empty we are, we feel intensely sorrowful.

2) *You mourn your own sin.* The reason for our poverty is our sin, by which we strive to live independent of God and run our own lives: "Sin is a complication of all evils. It is the spirits of mischief distilled. Sin dishonors God, it denies God's omniscience, it derides his patience, it distrusts his faithfulness."[17] Sin wants to justify your existence on the basis of attributes that make you better than other people—your race, your religion, your enlightened non-racism, your suffering, your powers of intelligence, your relative lack of overtly sinful behavior, your religious activism. You name it: you can feel superior because of it and think even God should be impressed.

This is why you should mourn not only your sin but your righteousness as well. Mourn your spiritual résumé—the one you have tried to beef up with every achievement you can possibly think of rather than with the righteousness that comes only from God. Mourn your sins of disobedience against God, mourn the folly of your overt rebellion against him, *and* mourn all the currency that you think you can offer God from your spiritual bank account. Look at all your righteous deeds—they are just filthy rags (Isaiah 64:6), so you should lament them.

3) *You mourn the sin of the world.* The kind of mourning Jesus means here must *begin* with feeling the offense of your own sin, but it moves quickly to grief over sin in general—sin that has corrupted

all human life, that makes all people poor in spirit, that causes all suffering and oppression in the world. You should cry over sexual trafficking, over pedophilia, over incest, over the oppression of the poor, over the African AIDS pandemic, over the oppression of women, over the affliction of the weak by unjust governments, over the occupation of conquering armies, over conscripting children into gruesome militias led by cruel warlords. If you truly grieve your own sin, you cannot help but grieve the sin all around you.

4) *You mourn the sin others commit against you.* You need only live in our world a little while before you see how sin has poisoned it thoroughly, probably because others will do or say things that hurt you deeply. Consider Isaiah 61, where the people of God mourned because captors oppressed them: their city was in ruins, and they were being dishonored. But they did not mourn simply because they had been sinned *against.* To think so makes too sharp a distinction between mourning because we are the *victims* of sin versus mourning because we are the *perpetrators* of sin. The whole book of Isaiah makes clear that Israel's oppressed condition was a consequence of their own foolishness, disobedience, and idolatry, which means that their sin and the sin of others against them are inextricably linked. Victim and victimizer are the *modus operandi* of every person, including the ancient Israelites.

5) *You mourn what all this sin has done to Jesus Christ.* We have all tasted the sting of our own sin, we have seen sin ravage our world—everyone mourns such stuff to some degree. But "gospel grief" is sorrow over how your sin grieves God (Jesus *died* for your sin) and how you murdered the Savior who loved you and has shown you such grace in the gospel (Jesus died for *your* sin). We should "weep bitterly over him, as one weeps over a firstborn" (Zechariah 12:10). Every other kind of grief is just plain grief; all other mourning is garden-variety mourning. But every true Christian has experienced the unique kind of grief that Zechariah described. It is a product of understanding the gospel of grace, and it is unlike anything else you have ever felt.

Gospel Grief in the Real World

When we mourn because of sin—our own sin, all sin generally in the world, specific sins others commit against us—we mourn comprehensively, broken over the practical atheism that afflicts every human being, for "all the suffering in the world stems from the sinful and self-destructive human tendency to act as if God did not exist."[18] To my mind, then, the mourning Jesus describes in the second beatitude is simply realism. Mourning is the only sane, reasonable response to seeing ourselves and the world as we really are.

Many people (including people in the church) think that Christianity teaches us to stick our heads in the sand and ignore just how miserable and difficult and fallen the world really is, wearing a perpetually silly grin on our faces. But the Bible is far more realistic than that. The Christian faith approaches life with wide-eyed realism. Do not ignore evil or suffering; instead, acknowledge it, see it for what it is, and mourn over it.

Of course, there are a lot of reasons why you might despise your sin. You might hate that you violated some standard you set for yourself that you never dreamed you could ever violate. Or you might dislike the potential consequences of your sin, like how you hurt others or how other people may now think less of you. You may feel bad because you did something contrary to what the Bible teaches. Or you might loathe yourself for so foolishly doing whatever you did. Many of these may be good reasons to mourn, but without the gospel, they are incomplete.

Christianity involves mourning over the great source of the entire world's misery—namely, sin, not least of which is my own. When you see the world as it really is and see yourself as you really are, you go to the depths of despair, and you will be crushed under the weight of it. Ironically, the only thing that keeps that despair from killing you is another form of mourning—what I have called "gospel grief." It works like this: if Christ had to *die* for my sins, then no matter what their effect on others or me, the greatest effect was on Christ, and I mourn the fact that I have sinned against such love. At that moment, I see the love of God for what it is, and I throw my hope completely on him. I lose the temptation to try to pull myself up by my bootstraps. I mourn away even my filthy rags of personal morality, because nothing can compensate for the pervasive poison of sin that killed my God. Every other kind of grief produces only death and despair, but gospel grief focuses my mourning (and any hope I have for comfort) on God himself.

Judas and Peter

We see the difference between crushing despair and gospel grief in two of the disciples: after the crucifixion of Jesus, Judas mourned sincerely but hopelessly, whereas Peter experienced gospel grief and, therefore, great blessing. In the first instance, the mourning crushed the mourner, but in the second, the mourning drove the mourner to Christ for mercy. Peter's mourning revealed his confident desperation for Jesus to help him in the way that only Jesus could, but Judas mourned in a Christ-less way, as though he was entirely beyond help.

Everyone knows Judas as the disciple who betrayed Jesus for money, but not many know (or remember) that Judas felt terrible for doing it. Matthew 27:3–4 says that when Judas saw what happened to Jesus, "he felt remorse and returned the thirty pieces of silver to the chief priests and elders, saying, 'I have sinned by betraying innocent blood.'" Judas took his sin seriously and had all the earmarks of proper remorse:[19]

- He saw his sin for what it was: the condemnation of Jesus.
- He admitted his sin specifically and with no excuses.
- He made restitution for his sin by returning the thirty pieces of silver.
- He acquitted Jesus of any guilt, calling him innocent.

Judas saw what his love of money did to Jesus—he saw that Jesus had to die for his materialism and greed. But there was one thing missing. What Judas did not see was Jesus dying *willingly* and indeed dying *for* sinners like him. He did not see Jesus as full of grace, love, and mercy. Thus, his guilt was too much for him: "he threw the pieces of silver into the temple sanctuary and departed; and he went away and hanged himself" (Matthew 27:5 NASB).

It is a good thing that Matthew gave us another picture of mourning to contrast with that one. Just before writing the story of Judas' Christless grief, Matthew wrote the story of another disciple's betrayal and grief. Peter denied Jesus three times, and when the rooster crowed, he remembered that Jesus said he would do just that; he therefore "went out and wept bitterly" (Matthew 26:75). That is, he went somewhere and cried his eyes out: he cried loudly with an overwhelming kind of grief. He was full of sorrow, and it showed. Like Judas, Peter betrayed Jesus, and like Judas, Peter felt deep remorse, but Peter did not kill himself. Instead, it seems that he moved forward with some kind of hope in Jesus. We know this because of how he reacted the next time he saw Jesus: when Peter realized that Jesus was standing on the shore while he was fishing, he threw himself in the water and swam to shore (John 21:1–8). Their boat was not far from the land—just a hundred yards away—but Peter could not wait to get to Jesus.

That is the difference between gospel grief and every other kind of grief. In the end, one runs *away* from Jesus and the other runs *toward* him. One looks at Jesus on the cross and focuses on how terrible the sin is that put him there, whereas the other focuses on how amazing the love is that willingly endured such suffering for my sin. Indeed, "The gospel creates the only kind of grief over sin which is clean and which does not crush."[20] Yes, we should mourn our sin, and not as an abstraction or simply because we broke God's rules or even because we ran our own lives; instead, we should mourn because we see our sin (and our righteousness) as our own personal murder weapon in the unjust execution of Jesus Christ who loved us so much. That kind of remorse will make you simultaneously hate your sin and love your Savior all the more.

John Newton captured these two facets of remorse in a hymn that is probably unfamiliar to you—for whatever reason, we do not seem to sing it much these days. These verses summarize the complex emotions that happen within us when we see the cross for what it is:

Thus while His death my sin displays
For all the world to view
(Such is the mystery of grace)

It seals my pardon too.
With pleasing grief and mournful joy
My spirit now is filled,
That I should such a life destroy,
Yet live by Him I killed.
                    – John Newton, "The Look"[21]

The cross reveals how terrible my sin is but also how sure my pardon is. When I see the terribleness of my sin, I feel deep grief that pleases both God and me as a grace-enlightened sinner—because it reveals that I have seen the cross for what it is. When I see my sure pardon, I feel deep joy, but not giddiness, for this joy cannot come without understanding that I am a murderer. I mourn the fact that I am responsible for killing that life on the tree, even as I delight in his death that gives me life. *Pleasing* grief and mournful *joy*—this is the grief of the gospel!

Perhaps this will be a new concept for you. After all, the Christian church is not characterized by mourning over sin. John Stott said that he thought this was because we overemphasize grace: "I fear that we evangelical Christians, by making much of grace, sometimes thereby make light of sin."[22] But I disagree. It is true that we evangelicals tend to make light of sin, but not because we have made much of grace. On the contrary, it is precisely because we *do not* understand grace and *have not* made much of it that we do not mourn our sin. Until you feel miserable for piercing Jesus with your sin, you have not really mourned; you only feel as miserable as you should when you see God's grace at work on and through the cross. If we understood grace, we would weep for our sins and the sins of others, and we would run to Jesus for help and hope.

True Comfort

If real mourning is gospel grief, then real comfort must come only from God himself *through* the gospel. The truly fortunate ones are those who have gospel grief, because the Lord himself comforts people with that kind of grief, and he comforts them with the exact same thing he used to elicit their mourning. That is, he comforts them with the knowledge that all their sin (and all its adverse effects in the world) has been overcome by the work of Jesus on the cross. The first question and answer of the Heidelberg Catechism puts it beautifully:

Question 1. What is thy only comfort in life and death?

Answer. That I with body and soul, both in life and death, am not my own, but belong unto my faithful Saviour Jesus Christ; who, with his precious blood, has fully satisfied for all my sins, and delivered me from all the power of the devil; and so preserves me that without the will of my heavenly Father, not a hair can fall from my head; yea, that all things must be subservient to my salvation, and therefore, by his Holy Spirit, He also assures me of eternal life, and makes me sincerely willing and ready, henceforth, to live unto him.

Through the gospel, Jesus allows those who mourn to experience the true comfort of grace right now. They do not have to wait for a time in the distant future to taste it. At the same time, the comfort that mourners experience now is only a partial realization of what they will know in the future when Jesus returns and consummates the kingdom of heaven. Then the Lord "will wipe away every tear from their eyes, and death shall be no more, neither shall there be mourning, nor crying, nor pain anymore" (Revelation 21:4). This is true comfort—comfort that we get to experience through the gospel in the present, and comfort that we get to experience in the future—by the sheer grace of God.

What Kind of Mourner Are You?

Are you miserable? Are you stricken with grief over sin—mourning all sin, but especially your own? If so, are you ridden with guilt and insecure? That could be a *good* thing! Not if you simply see your sin as failure to achieve a set of ethical norms or to live with good, Christian behavior, but it is good if you see your sin as that which nailed Jesus to the cross. Jesus loved you so much that he willingly stretched out his arms to suffer God's just wrath for you on the cross. Mourn your sin *and* rejoice in such comfort. Blessed are you who mourn like this, because you alone will be comforted.

Notably, Jesus does not say, "If you are sad enough, you will know the comfort of the gospel." He does not offer salvation by remorse but salvation by *grace*. You therefore cannot take any false hope in your own morality—not even in your own righteous indignation over your sin. What you have done to this God who loved you so much should humble you and move you to tears, and then to dependence upon him. Even the mourning itself is a gift, for you cannot work up true mourning for yourself. Celebrate Jesus because the gospel has shown you how horrible your sin is, yet how incapable you are of atoning for it. Celebrate Jesus because he comforts you perfectly in your mourning.

FOR YOUR HEAD

1. How do you explain the fact that we are not commanded to mourn but nevertheless need to be people who mourn in order to be citizens of the kingdom?
2. Describe how the first beatitude about being poor in spirit is related to the second beatitude about mourning.
3. How does understanding the gospel of grace produce the mourning that Jesus refers to in this beatitude? Why is that the only way to experience this kind of mourning?

FOR YOUR HEART

4. As you consider your life, how can you cultivate gospel grief in your daily routine?

FOR YOUR CHURCH

5. Mourning over our sin can produce in us fear, condemnation, and even a sense that we cannot possibly belong to God. How can we help each other if or when this happens?

FOR YOUR CITY

6. We certainly do not want our friends who are not yet Christians to get the impression from us that the Christian life is a life of misery. How can you be a person who mourns without being miserable?

4

THE GOOD NEWS OF HAVING NOTHING TO DEFEND

Speak softly and carry a big stick; you will go far.
— Theodore Roosevelt

Blessed are the meek, for they shall inherit the earth.
— Matthew 5:5

The meek will inherit the earth? The meek will rule the world? Jesus cannot be serious. His audience certainly would have known better. The overly submissive, compliant, spiritless, tame people of the world will never rule it. Take, for example, a survey of the Roman emperors or their regional governors, like Pontius Pilate, the magistrate in charge of Palestine in Jesus' lifetime. Unless you had a belly of steel, you simply could not ascend the ladder of the Roman political elite. And how about the Zealots? They were committed to violent overthrow of the Roman occupation and would have scoffed at Jesus' absurd notion that the meek would inherit the earth. So far, sitting on their hands had not helped the Jews get their homeland back under their own control, and the Zealots refused to endure oppression any longer. They knew that the meek just get stepped *on* and *over*. Enough was enough. Time to act.

The same is true in our culture. Meek people simply do not get the privilege of running things. They are the ones told what to do, and they do what they are told. They may not like getting pushed around, but they lack the gumption to do anything about it. So we use the word *meek* as an insult, preferring the sort of personal courage that says, "If it's to be, it's up to me."

This is not to say that we do not value humility in our world, for our culture does seem to admire those who know how to listen and have the self-control to keep quiet when it seems best to do so. We also decry ruthless dictators and savage rule breakers. We do not like modern-day Pontius Pilates who seek their own gain at whatever cost to underlings, and we prosecute Zealots—terrorists driven by idealism and willing to practice wanton violence. But at the same time, we think it downright wrong not to defend ourselves when mistreated or mistaken. We assume there is always something in us worth defending—some kernel of moral uprightness that others ought to respect. According to Jesus' definition, that means we are not meek.

Inheriting the Earth

The psalms promise that "the meek shall inherit the land and delight themselves in abundant peace" (Psalm 37:11), and ancient Jews put a lot of hope in that promise. They understood their inheritance to extend beyond the land of Canaan in Palestine to the whole earth, and they understood *abundant peace* as a time when God would finally put Israel's oppressors in their place and restore order to the whole universe (see Isaiah 66:22). But Jesus meant much more than that.

Jesus' original audience expected the meek to inherit the earth through an armed uprising led by their Messiah at the end of history. They were waiting for a big show in which their oppressors would be shattered like so many pots (see Psalm 2:8–9). But Jesus taught that the meek would experience their inheritance in the present: "the kingdom of heaven is *at hand*" (Matthew 4:17). After all, as we will see in chapter 9, God's children inherit first and foremost a *person*, not *property*. In the future, the whole earth will know that it is under the authority of King Jesus and his loyal subjects, and the Lord will make this known through his might. The property will be ours, and it will extend in every direction. In the meantime, we experience our inheritance of the earth through meekness—by taking refuge in God's unique son (Psalm 2:12), the one who receives his inheritance not by might but by virtue of his sonship (see Psalm 2:6–7).

This means that the only person who has earned the inheritance of the earth is Jesus, and he earned it by emptying himself (Philippians 2:7). Jesus fulfills all of the Law and the Prophets (Matthew 5:17), so all promises that the Old Testament makes to the meek belong to him. He is the meek one *par excellence* who inherits the earth and then shares his inheritance with all who put their faith in him (see Hebrews 9:15). His co-heirs have set aside all their so-called rights and gladly submitted themselves to God's rule as citizens of his kingdom. His co-heirs are meek like their Savior.

Gentle Jesus, Meek and Mild?

If Jesus is the only rightful heir of the earth, who gladly shares his inheritance with the meek, then we must look at Jesus to understand true meekness. Jesus called himself "gentle and lowly in heart" (Matthew 11:29), and he began the most triumphant week of his life by riding an unimpressive donkey, of all things, into the capital city (Matthew 21:5–7). But for Jesus, meekness definitely did not mean spiritless compliance, sitting around waiting for someone else to do something. Charles Wesley's hymn "Gentle Jesus, Meek and Mild" suggests that if we could but emulate Jesus, we would be sweet and compliant children of God, but it seems to miss the kind of aggressive meekness Jesus actually embodied.

Remember Jesus getting upset in the temple (Matthew 21:12–13)? Here is "gentle Jesus" acting like a lunatic. He entered the temple and wreaked havoc with the money-changers. He drove people out of the temple and turned over tables, coins flying everywhere, animals bleating, people running chaotically while he quoted the Scriptures to them. Then, in Matthew 23, he leveled incendiary and inflammatory accusations against the scribes and Pharisees, calling them sons of hell, hypocrites, and serpents (see verses 29–33 especially). But not even his dearest disciples were safe from harsh words when they seemed appropriate. In Matthew 16:23, Jesus called his closest friend the devil, which might today be like comparing someone to Hitler or Bin Laden and *meaning* it. Jesus Christ—the paragon of meekness—went ballistic in the temple, spoke curses against his elders, and rebuked his only friends.

It might seem, then, as if "gentle Jesus, meek and mild" is the greatest misnomer ever! In fact, we may begin to wonder whether Jesus was truly meek at all. We think of meek people as humbly patient, especially when provoked. Meek people do not take matters into their own hands, nor do they lash out in fits of anger, but it seems like he did just that both in the temple and when he rebuked the religious leaders and even Peter. The church has historically seen Jesus as so docile and domesticated that we find it hard to interpret these stories. But do not ignore the obvious reality of Jesus' robust meekness.

In point of fact, meekness does not mean avoiding conflict or refusing to call a spade a spade just because the consequences seem undesirable. Meekness simply means never asserting itself for its own sake. You can be meek while correcting or rebuking or admonishing—just not if you do those things as expressions of one-upmanship or personal defensiveness. Jesus was no indecisive pushover,[23] nor did he have a spirit of compromise,[24] but he was radically meek. He shows us that meekness is not conflict-avoidance or being agreeable just for the sake of being agreeable. Meekness is not milquetoast.

Not for a single moment did Jesus do anything for the purpose of personal self-defense, as if he felt threatened by other people. Neither did he ever do anything to assume a position of superiority over his rivals or to serve his own pride. But he did confront falsehood with strong actions and words—the stakes were too high to ignore it. Everything Jesus did in his life was an expression of his deep humility and profound desire to obey his Father and put others first. *That* is true meekness.

Get Meekness Through Poverty and Mourning

If Jesus never defended himself or felt threatened by others or assumed a position of authority over his rivals, then I am in trouble when it comes to meekness. Jesus had every right to do those things, but he did not because he was meek; I have little to no right to do those things, but I do them anyway. So how do I get meekness? Take two steps backwards and think about the beautiful internal logic of the Beatitudes: if you are meek, you are first a poor mourner.

If you are poor in spirit, you understand your utter dependence upon God—how spiritually insolvent you are before the Lord. You know that you have nothing to give God but your liabilities; whatever achievements and goodness you thought you had are filthy rags in God's sight (see Isaiah 64:6 NIV), for even your best stuff has been corrupted by your sinfulness. You see how much Jesus paid for your sin—the ransom of his life, suffering and dying on the cross to take God's wrath for sin as your substitute.

So you grieve over the sin that cost God so much and that made you that destitute before God. You weep over the sin and self-reliance that put you (and the rest of the world) in such dire straits. Chiefly, you mourn the fact that by your sin *you* nailed Jesus to the cross. You know that your self-reliance did horrible things to the Lord who loved you, so when you see Jesus dying on the cross, you weep that he *had* to die for you, and you weep because he *willingly* died for you as an expression of his love. Meekness seems like a natural product of such understanding: poverty of spirit makes you mourn your sin, and mourning your sin makes you meek.

Meekness is an internal attitude that you see externally as you relate with other people. If mourning is the *emotional* counterpart to poverty of sprit, then meekness is the *relational* counterpart to both poverty of sprit and mourning. When we see ourselves in the light of who God is, we understand our poverty of spirit and mourn.

But when that self-assessment translates into our relationships with other people, it looks like meekness and gentleness.[25]

Practice Meekness as Non-Defensiveness and Deference

If you see yourself as a poor, miserable sinner, you will be gentle with others because you understand that they are sinners just like you are (see Hebrews 5:1–2). Even when others mistreat you and wrongly accuse you, you will treat them with gentleness because meekness means that when the accusation has no basis, we will not move to defend ourselves. We do not feel the need to justify ourselves against accusations that amount to little more than personal attacks. We will bear injuries well. As one Puritan writer says, "A meek spirit, like wet tinder, will not easily take fire,"[26] and what makes us "wet tinder" is the deep knowledge that we are as bad as everyone thinks we are: even if that particular attack does not hit the mark precisely, we know what we are capable of, so we do not defend ourselves for our own sakes.

Rather, when others perceive and then call out our weaknesses and flaws, meekness will drive us to accept accusations with humility. We know that we really are as bad as (if not worse than) they say we are. So the meek are quick to consider whatever truth may reside in an attack. When you see yourself as bankrupt before God, then whatever accusations come your way will seem at least partly reasonable to you.[27] When someone suggests that you are a sinner or foolish or ignorant, it makes perfect sense to you because you know how poor in spirit you are. Think about it: if someone accused me of being Bob Glenn, I would not make excuses or justify myself. Why not? Because I am Bob Glenn, for better and for worse—mostly worse. If I am who they say I am, I do not defend myself but simply acknowledge the truth.

Similarly, meekness resists the temptation to assert oneself. We feel almost irresistibly inclined to do this with others who have power over us, especially when they exert that power for their own misguided purposes. That power may be real or merely perceived, but when we sense a power struggle, we want to attack first—to go on the offensive in our own defense. So we tout our accomplishments, show off, and compare ourselves with others in an attempt to lift ourselves up by putting them down. We may do this before the perceived opponent ever shows sign of an attack if we fear losing face.

I saw this so clearly in myself one morning at a coffee shop when the fittest man I know suddenly walked in. We work out at the same gym and talk somewhat regularly about diet and exercise. This guy is in his mid-forties, and you can see every one of his muscles all year long. On this particular day, he walked into the coffee shop while I was eating . . . a doughnut. As soon as I saw him, my mind raced to how I might justify such a sacrilege. He hadn't seen me or said anything to me, and I certainly did not plan to alert him to my presence, but my mind was racing about what I would tell him about my doughnut if he said hello—how I would justify my Homer Simpson indulgence. "This is my sweet thing for the week" might work. Or how about "I'm breaking my diet to give my metabolism a boost"? He had not attacked, but I perceived him as someone with power over me, so I loaded my defensive gun. I wanted to be ready—to assert and defend myself—before he had the chance to reveal my weakness and his strength.

We all work this way. When we feel like someone thinks less of us or will think less of us or is about to think less of us, we make more of ourselves. It is a defense mechanism by which we try to avoid our own weaknesses or at least pretend that they do not control us. But meekness frees us to say, "There is nothing to defend." Not because we feel justified in whatever we are doing but because our mournful poverty of spirit has brought us to the place where we actually believe we have nothing within us to defend. "I am just a sinner" is not a pitiful thing to say but the truest thing to say about ourselves.

Meekness must, therefore, involve self-control, "freedom from malice and a vengeful spirit,"[28] and the absence of pretension. Meekness assumes that I have the power to retaliate, to defend or else assert myself, to claim my own rights, but choose to bridle my impulses and allow myself to be defamed and defrauded. More than this, because I do not need to defend myself, I will not behave maliciously or vengefully; instead, I will practice patience and understanding with others as fellow sinners on the journey, for there is no pretense in the meek. We have already renounced our own supposed goodness and spirituality,[29] so we do not need to pretend to be something we are not. We can afford to be honest and forthright about our weaknesses, limitations, and sins in our relationships with other people—in fact, we can embrace them. We can rest in our great defender who will come to our aid if and when needed.

Jesus did just that, revealing supreme meekness during his trial and crucifixion. He never defended himself against false accusations even though no one could make any legitimate complaint of sin in him or reasonably defame his character. Jesus was unjustly accused, tried, and executed, and he *never* asserted himself or defended his honor. He refused to use his power to his own advantage even in those final horrendous hours and instead trusted in his Father alone for his eventual vindication. But Jesus' meekness is different than ours. He endured accusation meekly not because of any weakness, flaw, or sin on his part—he had none! There is a sense, then, in which our meekness is much easier than his because we actually have nothing in us worth defending. If we saw ourselves rightly, we should be amazed that God and others do not treat us more poorly than they do.[30]

So meekness will, on the one hand, keep you from defending yourself (because you know that there is nothing in you worth defending), and it will, on the other hand, drive you to put others first. The gospel reveals to you that you are not morally superior to anyone else, and also that you need not fear other people any longer. This means that you can actually love others now. As long as people are a threat to you—to your reputation, your standing, or your status—you cannot look out for their interests before your own. But meekness removes that threat because you know that no one else can ever tell you anything that your heavenly Father does not already know about you. Meekness, therefore, translates into a desire to spend yourself completely so that others may experience great good (see Philippians 2:5–8).[31]

Gospel Meekness

The luckiest people in the world are those who refuse to defend themselves and resolve to put others first, for these people—and only these people—will inherit the earth. But we cannot add enough relational excellence to our spiritual résumés to claim that inheritance. Inheritances do not work that way. Neither is Jesus advising us to attempt that, for the Beatitudes are not commands. Rather, the Beatitudes take our gospel temperature: they are a gauge to see if and how well we understand God's grace. The only way that meekness can become part of your character is if you understand the gospel.

You may be able to acknowledge your own poverty of spirit and mourn over your sin before God, but to respond with meekness when other people tell you how they have seen your sin in you is another story.[32] I see how difficult meekness is when I confess sin to others in general terms, reluctant to get specific. I also see this in my ability to handle self-criticism gracefully while I handle criticism from others defensively. You might *think* that you have come to grips with your spiritual bankruptcy before God and mourned over how you have grieved him and murdered his Son, but you have not really understood if you do not then demonstrate meekness. And the proof of your meekness is in how you relate to your brother whom you can see (1 John 4:20).

Maybe you are morally consistent in many areas, such that it seems unfair when others point out deficiencies in other areas; in fact, it seems more justified that you should point out to others where they fail. But the gospel shows you how utterly indefensible you are: just look at Jesus dying on the cross for you. If you are so sinful and self-centered and self-reliant as to require the Son of God to die on a cross for your salvation, then you really have nothing in yourself worth defending. Understanding the depth of your own sin makes you gentle with others (remember Hebrews 5:1–2).

But Christians have another good reason to give up defending themselves, and that is because someone else has become our defender. I am safe in the gospel. Even though God knows that I am a bankrupt, vile sinner, he has accepted and loved me. Because of this,

I am liberated from the need to defend myself, to make excuses, to put others down and gossip about them, to make myself out as more than I am. Those things make me feel more secure in my flesh, but I do not need that kind of security anymore.

Meekness is thus a significant litmus test for whether you really understand the gospel. Are you poor in spirit? Have you mourned? Do you understand grace? For grace does not simply change how you think of yourself, or how you think of God, or even how you think of yourself with respect to God. Grace changes how you relate to other people. The certainty of the Lord's loving acceptance of sinners through the gospel gives us the freedom to love and serve others rather than compare ourselves with them or defend ourselves from them. You can embrace your weaknesses and celebrate your flaws precisely because you know that you have nothing worth defending, and much more than that, because you know that Jesus loves you in spite of them. Indeed, he died to defend you forever as his co-heir and friend. You can now celebrate your weaknesses—not as flaws per se but as the means by which God's flawless grace shines in your life. Only understanding the grace of God can make you meek.

FOR YOUR HEAD

1. Explain "the how, the when, and the who" of this beatitude. How does Jesus change the preconceived notions of his audience?
2. How do you explain the fact that Jesus does not command us to be meek, yet we must be meek in order to have citizenship in God's kingdom?
3. How is meekness linked to the first two beatitudes about poverty of spirit and mourning?
4. What does it mean to be meek?

FOR YOUR HEART

5. Give an example of a time you defended yourself even when you may have been in the wrong. What did you want to protect?

6. How does understanding the gospel of grace help you resist the temptation to defend yourself even when you do not think you did anything wrong?
7. Can you name people or types of people that you fear because they have power over you? Who and why? How does believing the gospel change that?

FOR YOUR CHURCH

8. Give an example of a time when you lashed out in anger toward someone or retaliated against someone who said something offensive about you?
9. How can understanding this beatitude help you when you feel the need to defend yourself or "take somebody down" when someone confronts you or makes you look bad?

FOR YOUR CITY

10. It seems like a disposition of meekness could do more to change our non-Christian friends' understanding of Christianity than anything else. Do you agree or disagree? Discuss how seeing meekness could change a non-Christian's attitude and assumptions about the Christian faith.

5

THE GOOD NEWS OF YOUR STARVATION

You don't understand! I coulda had class! I coulda been
a contender. I coulda been somebody instead of a bum,
which is what I am.

> – Terry Malloy, *On the Waterfront*

Blessed are those who hunger and thirst for righteousness,
for they shall be satisfied.

> – Matthew 5:6

Have you ever wondered why it took so long for Brett Favre, the
most decorated, record-breaking, record-holding quarterback in
the history of the NFL to hang it up? He announced his retirement two or three times (depending on who does the counting) before
he actually retired, but I think the reason he had a hard time following through was because he regarded football as his righteousness.
He could not fathom what else he might do, and he believed that he
needed continued success in football to remain acceptable to himself
and to others. Football justified his existence.

Most of us think of happiness the same way: we are satisfied
when and only when we have achieved something worthwhile. Our

happiness may center on our careers or our relationships or our body image, but we are unhappy until we have what we want, and when we get it, we never want to let it go. We will do whatever it takes to hang onto it for as long as possible, even if we might be able to exchange it for something with similar (or even greater) satisfaction—like, say, retirement from a time-consuming career. When we feel in control of our righteousness, we will continually debate the "what ifs" of trading that satisfying thing for something else that may give us more pleasure. If we are like Brett Favre, it will take a long time before we take a step in a new direction, if we ever do.

At the end of the day, it's the having, not the hungering, that defines satisfaction in our world. We definitely do not think of ourselves as happy when we *long* for something we do not yet own. Only those who have what they want are satisfied, and we pity the needy. We feel ashamed if we lack anything and celebrate self-sufficiency. But in this beatitude, Jesus again offers counterintuitive logic: happy and full are those who starve.

Hungering or Having?

Jesus seems to presume that hungering and thirsting are preferable to *having*, but wouldn't you prefer a full belly to an empty one? And surely those who are *already* righteous are blessed, not those who only *wish* they were righteous. The Old Testament teaches this throughout (see Psalm 5:12 and 106:3, for example), and common sense tells us the same thing. Jesus says the opposite, though: Neither those who think they have attained righteousness[33] nor "the bloated,"[34] but those who *long* for righteousness—they are the happy ones.

Have you ever longed for anything? When Jesus mentions hungering and thirsting, he does not mean something like the rumble you might feel in your stomach around dinnertime. He means starvation and dying of thirst. Most who read this book will probably have a hard time identifying with real hunger and thirst (though that is certainly not true for everyone), but in the ancient world, many people lived on the brink of starvation and even traveled the desert for extended periods of time without any water at all. That is the picture when

Jesus speaks this beatitude. He is talking about a desperate longing to be fed—a profound yearning for righteousness. He calls that the most blessed place to be: the place where you know that you do not have righteousness and where you know that you are desperate for it.

The people of Israel had been there before: "hungry and thirsty, their soul fainted within them" (Psalm 107:5), and God helped them because of his steadfast love for them. In that instance, they longed for rescue from the wilderness, and he led them to a city they could call home, "For he satisfies the longing soul, and the hungry soul he fills with good things" (Psalm 107:9). Problem solved, right? They were hungry, and then God satisfied their hunger.

But the psalmist goes on to recount how the Israelites found themselves in need again and again: they would long for rescue from oppression, and then they would long for rescue from death, and then they would long for rescue from natural disaster. The psalmist even wrote a refrain for how they continually asked for help, how they so often "cried to the LORD in their trouble, and he delivered them from their distress" (Psalm 107:6, 13, 19, 28). They knew that God alone was their hope in whatever dire circumstance they found themselves, and they frequently found themselves hungry for one thing or another, asking him to satisfy their longings.

Jesus means to evoke that same pattern of longing and satisfaction in this beatitude—desperate and recurring, continual and confident longing until complete satisfaction comes in the next age. God has satisfied his people in the past, but never completely. Even now, Jesus has inaugurated the kingdom of God, but it is not fully consummated yet. So when Jesus promises satisfaction here, he means that we can *taste* the fullness of the kingdom, and we can have that taste *right now*. That taste makes us hunger and thirst for it all the more—desperate for the kingdom to come in all its glory. We can even now come into our inheritance precisely because we hunger and thirst for it.

Total Perfection

But what exactly does Jesus mean by *righteousness*? Jesus says we are blessed when we hunger and thirst because we will be satisfied, and we have begun to understand what he means by that longing and that satisfaction, but what exactly are we hungering for? The word *righteousness* appears throughout the Bible, and Jesus refers to it often in the Sermon on the Mount, so we need to get a handle on it.

First, we must see that righteousness means that you do right things. A righteous person consistently practices behavior that reflects God's will.[35] You might think of righteousness as a reputation that gets you into God's presence.[36] To be *righteous* means that you have lived the kind of life that God finds acceptable. How much right living do you need to justify your existence? Jesus says that to enter God's kingdom, you must have more righteousness than the religious leaders during his day had (Matthew 5:20). In comparison with them, do you have what it takes to be acceptable to God?

Even if you have never asked this question quite so theologically, you have probably considered your righteousness relative to people around you. Think about it: if you have ever wondered whether you have what it takes to please someone, you have wondered about your righteousness. We all want to be received or accepted by those whose opinions and decisions matter most to us. We want to do right, however we define that. What must you do—or whose approval must you have—to know that your life is worth something? Righteousness is whatever you look to in order to justify your existence, and we all look to something. Maybe you can identify with one of these common pursuits:

- Doing your work well as a parent, employer, employee, or homemaker.
- Being competent, capable, wise, and thorough—an expert in your field.
- Having scholarly achievements, or being shrewd enough not to care about such things.
- Being regarded as physically attractive.
- Achieving the wisdom of age and life experience.
- Practicing generosity and/or living below your means.

- Not getting noticed, not causing waves, not making hassles for others.
- Being nice, kind, and sweet with people, not losing your cool but having an even temper with everyone.
- Suffering psychological problems, trials, or hard knocks.
- Being cool, stylish, funny, witty, or sophisticated.
- Practicing cleanliness, neatness, and orderliness.
- Having a certain family of origin or ethnicity.
- Loving your friends and family with loyalty.

Think about what really moves you to get up and do your daily life; that will reveal what you think makes your life worth living. And if you want to test whether you bank your hope on true righteousness or something lesser, look at what you get the most defensive about. For example, if your righteousness is your own competency, then you will fight with someone who suggests you made a mistake. You will attack your accuser and defend yourself or else become deeply embittered, depressed, or devastated. You may feel shocked and lash out in fierce anger against someone who dares question you. Ultimately, you know that you do not have what it takes, but if your self-righteousness gets exposed as counterfeit, your life as you know it is over. So you desperately defend your righteousness.

But the righteousness that Jesus means for you to want is something altogether different than anything you could accomplish on your own. He means righteousness as living rightly in God's sight so consistently and perfectly that God accepts you. We know that Jesus means comprehensive righteousness because Matthew records an unusual Greek construction here: instead of using the customary genitive form, Jesus puts the phrase "for righteousness" in the accusative, which means that Jesus is talking about not just *some* righteousness but all the righteousness in the world.[37]

It adds up to this: the only record of right-doing that can gain you audience with God and satisfy your heart is a comprehensively perfect record. You must live a life that God finds completely right. Jesus says this straightforwardly later in this chapter: "Be perfect," he says, "as your heavenly Father is perfect" (Matthew 5:48). Of course, you know from all of your failed attempts at lower standards of righteousness that this is impossible. Maybe that's why you must long for it rather than achieve it. Jesus wants you to hunger and thirst for a perfect record and a perfect life—nothing less.

Can't Get No Satisfaction

It should come as no surprise that the only standard of righteousness that the holy God accepts is perfection. You would expect nothing less from the "holy, holy, holy" Lord (Isaiah 6:3). What may surprise you is what Jesus is *not* saying. He is not saying that you need to achieve this kind of righteousness in order to be acceptable to God. He is saying something far more radical. He is actually saying that you cannot *achieve* this righteousness but can only *receive* it as a gift.

How can a person who hungers and thirsts (who is dehydrated and starving) achieve anything on his own? If you are starving, you don't plant a garden; you need food now, so you cry out for it. If you are dying of thirst, you don't dig a well; you beg for water. You need someone with food and water to have mercy on you and satisfy your hunger and thirst. You need someone to *give* you the food and water you need lest you die.

This is the picture Jesus paints with this beatitude. He wants us to see that a person who understands grace is a person who has seen his empty spiritual stomach and parched spiritual throat and realized that unless someone intervenes to give him what he needs, he will not survive. He knows that unless the Lord gives him his own righteousness as a gift, he cannot hope to be satisfied. And this gift of righteousness comes only through the righteousness of Christ. As the Apostle Paul puts it in 2 Corinthians 5:21: "For our sake he [God] made him [Jesus] to be sin who knew no sin, so that in him we might become the righteousness of God."

The Glory of Double Imputation

Jesus wants you to exchange your self-righteousness for his true righteousness because he knows that he and he alone can and will satisfy. You cannot enjoy God's presence with anything less, neither will God accept anything less. What he must have in mind, then, is what theologians call *double imputation*—God attributes your sins and guilt to Christ while he attributes Christ's righteousness and innocence to you.

Most Christians are comfortable with the first part of that definition. They understand that when Jesus died, he died for our sins. They believe that our sins were withdrawn from our account and credited to his and that the Father punished his son for those sins. But few Christians consider the other side of imputation—namely, that even as our sins were credited to Jesus' account, his comprehensively perfect righteous life was credited to ours.

Think of it like this: if your spiritual bank account was overdrawn 30 billion dollars and Jesus paid off all of your creditors by taking your sins on his shoulders, you would have no debt whatsoever. Tremendous! You could not have hoped to repay the debt you owed, and a third party paid it off? No wonder the psalmist says, "Blessed is the one whose transgression is forgiven, whose sin is covered" (Psalm 32:1). But God does one better: now that your financial situation has been brought to a zero bottom line, your heavenly Father deposits into your account all the money in the world by taking the perfect, sinless life of greatness that Jesus lived, and crediting it to your account. This money will never run out, nor will it suffer risk in the market or in an economic recession: your account is eternally full of all the righteousness you would ever need. You don't have to look any longer for ways to earn credits with God because your bank account is already filled to overflowing with the perfectly righteous life of your Savior, Jesus Christ!

Jesus Alone Has What It Takes

Some people get worried, though, about resting in that blessedness. God has wired us for righteousness, and the only sort suitable to God is the perfect righteousness of Christ. He will gladly and freely give it to us so that we never have any want again, but not many

Christians operate with Jesus' righteousness as the platform of their acceptance with God. We rarely act on the belief that Jesus and Jesus alone has "what it takes" to open up the way into the presence of God. We do not actively and continually rest in Christ's righteousness, so we make something else for ourselves. We take the road of moralism.

When we see that we lack righteousness, one of our first impulses is to try to make up for it ourselves. This is the righteousness of panic, adding more Bible-reading and sermon-listening and church-going to our calendars because we think, "I need to get my act together! I am a mess and I need to do something about it." But righteousness is not religious respectability.[38] Christianity is not moralism. We desperately need a righteousness that is not our own, and Jesus offers it to us through the gospel. He gives his perfect life as a gift to those who hunger and thirst for it.

You do not need Jesus simply as your example. You do not need Jesus merely as your helper. You need Jesus ultimately as your Savior! You do not need reformation. You need rescue. And Jesus is the great rescuer—not of non-Christians only but also of Christians. Those who belong to Jesus know for sure that they are not perfect, which makes them press forward all the more earnestly into Jesus (Philippians 3:12). Only Christians know that the thing they so desperately need is the righteousness of Jesus, and they want to receive that gift anew every day. Christians need continual rescue.

We are the ones who wake up with sins to confess. We continually feel our poverty of spirit and continue to mourn our sin, seeing more and more clearly how we have nothing within ourselves worth defending. But if you wallow in your remaining sin, you have missed the point. Instead, as you grow in grace, you begin every day banking all your hope anew on the righteousness of Christ. If you continually remind yourself that you are accepted completely and solely because of the comprehensively perfect righteousness of Christ, then you can be confident that he will never reject you. Jesus and Jesus alone has what it takes for you, yesterday and today and always.

The Promise of Satisfaction

Jesus makes a marvelous promise to those who hunger and thirst for his righteousness: "they shall be satisfied." No other kind of righteousness can satisfy your soul's longing for acceptance with God; it will only make you miserable. Every other kind of righteousness works hard to deceive you into believing that your belly is full, that you do not need the righteousness of Christ, that you are perfectly fine, and that if you are lacking, you need only add a little bit of Jesus to make your own righteousness more fulfilling—Jesus becomes icing on the cake.

We want to take credit for our record, to bring some righteousness to God rather than assume the humiliating position of a starving beggar receiving a handout from our maker. But to whatever extent you fail to rest in Christ's righteousness, to that extent you will be unsatisfied. Counterfeit righteousness will only make you miserable. Justifying your existence with anything outside of Christ is like drinking salt water: it will only make you thirstier.[39] But looking to Christ as your righteousness will be like a cool, clear, clean glass of spring water quenching your deepest thirst.

This is how we make sense of the fact that Christians simultaneously experience deep satisfaction and deep dissatisfaction. The gospel tells us that Jesus can satisfy our hunger and our thirst, and Jesus does satisfy us. But satisfaction *in* Christ begets hunger *for* Christ. Christianity never says, "I have arrived. I am happy with where I am." If you feel content with your current righteousness, you no longer are feasting at the table of Christ's righteousness. Instead, each satisfying gulp makes me see more clearly my great poverty of spirit, so I mourn that and see myself as no better than anyone else, which means I never stop hungering and thirsting for righteousness. Imagine being able to enjoy the greatest meal you ever ate indefinitely, over and over and over again. You eat it, find yourself satisfied, and immediately you want to eat it again—and you get to do just that. We are perfectly satisfied in Jesus, and we are at the same time continually dissatisfied because we see in the cross our lack of food and drink—our lack of righteousness—so we continue to see our ongoing need for Jesus' righteousness.

The Gospel and Hungering and Thirsting for Righteousness

I wrote previously that to whatever extent you fail to rest in Christ's righteousness, to that extent you will be unsatisfied. The opposite is also true. To whatever extent you remember and rejoice in the work of Jesus on your behalf, to that extent you will be blessedly satisfied. You will deepen and increase your hunger for righteousness when you see the righteousness of God displayed on the cross, because there you see the desperateness of your condition and the completeness of Christ's righteousness. On the cross, God emptied your account of sin, transferred it all to Jesus, and made Jesus pay what you owe him; and on the cross, God filled your account with Jesus' comprehensively perfect righteousness, transferred it all to you, never to make you pay him back. How could you want anything else?

This is the Beatitude of the Beatitudes—a profound summary of what the Christian faith is all about. You no longer need to search for something to justify your existence: if you are a Christian, you have all the righteousness you will ever need. You never need to wake up wondering whether God accepts you. You never need to worry about what will happen when you fail in your faithfulness. You are secure if Jesus is your righteousness. Your account bursts with righteousness, and you will never start any day in a deficit. Rather, every day is a surplus! You will continue to mourn your poverty of spirit and see your meekness more clearly, but that will just make you hunger and thirst all the more for the righteousness Jesus has deposited in your account.

Christianity is not about making yourself Christian.[40] It is about ceasing and desisting from the futile and foul attempt to save yourself by your own record or merit or background. It is about repenting of your righteousness to embrace the righteousness of Christ—and it is about doing this every day. Are you satisfied in the righteousness of Christ or are you still trying to make yourself a Christian—to work up your own righteousness? Are you satisfied with the righteousness of Christ or are you smug and self-satisfied, self-congratulatory, hypersensitive, or defensive? Do you find yourself more and more free from "self-concern, pride, boasting, self-protection, sensitiveness"[41] and whatever else concerns you in the flesh? Then you are growing more and more in your satisfaction with the righteousness of Christ. You long for righteousness. You are bent on getting it. In fact, you have found some, and you are banking on it. The question is whose righteousness is it? If you come to Christ's table having already stuffed yourself with your own righteousness, you will starve yourself and never know the satisfaction of the gospel. But if you come to the table with an appetite for Christ's righteousness, it is yours. Bring your appetite and feast at the table of the comprehensively perfect righteousness of Christ, and you will be satisfied.

FOR YOUR HEAD

1. Explain what Jesus' original audience would have thought about the idea that you are blessed if you hunger and thirst for righteousness.
2. List several things you have learned in this chapter about what righteousness means.

FOR YOUR HEART

3. Think specifically about what you defend in yourself, especially when others point out apparent weaknesses. Name at least two of your sensitive spots.
4. Your answer above will indicate what you think it takes to please others or God. What do you look to other than Christ for your righteousness? Give examples.

FOR YOUR CHURCH

5. How can this beatitude help others at your church or small group who are guilt-ridden and insecure in their walk with Jesus?
6. What questions can we ask each other to determine if we are getting our righteousness from ourselves or if we are growing in our understanding of Christ's comprehensively perfect righteousness, regularly re-receiving it as his gift to us?

FOR YOUR CITY

7. How would you explain to someone who has little understanding of Christianity the paradox of the banquet table Jesus sets for his brothers and sisters? That is, how would you explain to someone that those who come to Christ's table with an appetite for his righteousness will be satisfied, but those who come stuffed with their own righteousness will never know the satisfaction that comes through Jesus?

6

THE GOOD NEWS OF EXPENSIVE CHARITY

I stick my neck out for nobody.
— Rick, *Casablanca*

Blessed are the merciful, for they shall receive mercy.
— Matthew 5:7

D o you value mercy? Or do you prefer vengeance and retribution? We tend to celebrate those who finish off their enemies or who at least hold grudges. We may say that we have forgiven offenses, but we certainly feel justified never to forget them, even relishing the fact that we have grudges to hold. Perhaps the high divorce rate in America speaks to this heart reality, for to be sure, forgiveness seems like a rare commodity in our world. More than that, we lack generosity when it comes to the material side of mercy. We can practice some measure of mercy to the poor, but only after we take care of ourselves. Rarely do we find ourselves giving the best and first of what we have to help those in need.

This is not to say that our world places no value on being merciful, because it does. Philanthropy is an important part of American culture. In fact, the Twin Cities (where I live) routinely come up among the top cities in the nation where people are involved with volunteer organizations that help people. But I wonder how many of those involved with such charitable causes choose to feel the effects of others' burdens. How many will go without something for themselves (like, say, retirement money) in order to give it generously to others? It was not uncommon for early Christians to fast for two or three days and to save what they would have spent or used for food in order to meet the needs of the other Christians and unbelievers around them.[42] Have you ever heard of anyone doing that today? Has the thought ever crossed your mind to do so?

Honestly, mercy is hard. Even for God.

What Mercy Cost

From before the creation of the world, God was on a quest to pour out mercy to sinners, and that quest involved the life and death and resurrection of his eternal son. Jesus went through the most difficult ordeal ever conceived to bring about our reconciliation with God: the Father delivered him over to his own wrath for our sin. On the cross, Jesus experienced in his body the eternal punishment we all deserved—all of God's holy, furious, merciless hatred for all of our self-absorption and self-pity and self-reliance.

When Jesus was delivered to the Father's wrath, he experienced a form of abandonment that he had never known before. When Jesus said with the psalmist, "My God, my God, why have you forsaken me?" (Matthew 27:46), he expressed unparalleled dereliction—abandonment like no one else ever has or will experience. He and his father enjoyed the deepest possible intimacy because they existed together as father and son from all eternity, so when that relationship was interrupted, the loss was devastating. But Jesus voluntarily drank the cup of God's wrath so that you and I could bathe in God's mercy.

You may not want to think that you are as bad as all that, thinking that Jesus went to more trouble than was necessary. But it is worse than you know—only Jesus knows how bitter that cup was, and he sweat blood just thinking about it. What is more, Jesus *willingly* experienced the deepest possible pain so that he could magnify his Father's glory by drawing sinners into relationship with him. He was not compelled to do it. He loved his Father and us—weak, flawed, sinful, self-righteous, self-serving, self-reliant people—so much that he gladly endured God's wrath for us (see Hebrews 12:2). This is the mercy of the Christian God. And those who have received his mercy show others the same.

The Gospel Is Mercy

Mercy, as distinct from grace, refers to God seeing us in the misery of sin and being moved by that misery to do something about it: "Grace is especially associated with men in their sins; mercy is especially associated with men in their misery."[43] Indeed, sin has made us miserable, and God exercises mercy when he rescues us from our present and inevitable future misery. We are lonely, isolated, aimless, clueless, and willfully ignorant, without meaning or purpose in life. We are subject to all kinds of physical suffering, victims of the cruelty of others and the apparent capriciousness of a natural order gone awry. And Americans specialize in some particular miseries: we are depressed, discouraged, anxious, addicted, angry, controlled by lust, overweight, and in debt.

Whatever your particular experience, you can be sure of this: human beings suffer all kinds of miseries as a result of sin, but God has mercy on us. He sees us in our misery of sin, squirming in our blood (see Ezekiel 16 for this wonderful illustration of the Lord's mercy), and he is moved not only to *feel* compassion but also to actively relieve our misery. We made the bed we lie in, and God knows it—our misery is a consequence of our own sin—but God hates to see us like that, so he visits us with the greatest mercy the world has ever known, which is the Lord Jesus Christ. As John the Baptist's father said, Jesus came as an expression of the "tender mercy of our God" (Luke 1:78).

The subject of mercy comes up often in Matthew's gospel, both in what Jesus *says* (see 5:43–48; 9:13; 12:7; 18:21–35; 23:23; 25:31–46) and in what Jesus *does* (see 9:27–31; 15:21–28; 17:14–18; 20:29–34). In fact, this gospel sounds a lot like the Old Testament in its declarations and demonstrations of God's mercy,[44] but Jesus called attention to God's radical mercy toward *all* people, "not only those on the fringes of society but even enemies."[45] Whether considering enemies (Matthew 5:43–48) or disabled persons (9:1–8), Jesus took the same two-fold approach to mercy: it is pardon *and* kindness,[46] forgiveness *and* compassion.[47] Jesus' mercy always included a non-physical component (pardon/forgiveness) and a physical component (kindness/compassion).

Jesus revealed this robust mercy throughout his life and practiced it to its fullest extent on the cross. There, on Calvary, Jesus poured out mercy to sinners. And if we have received his mercy, we will become a conduit for that mercy to flow through us to others, materially and immaterially. This means that our mercy toward others must involve charity *and* forgiveness.

In One Hand of Mercy, We Find Charity

What do you think of when you hear the word *charity*: organizations that help needy people? For most of us, our primary involvement with charity as such is to give money (if we have extra) or goods (when we declutter) so that nonprofits can then distribute our wealth and stuff to people who have less. For most of us, *charity* is something we do in a clean and distant way. And most of you reading this book probably will not think of yourselves as the objects of charity. But that is exactly how God sees you: a big charity case. He became just like you to extend charity toward you, so that you would do the same for others.

Think about how charitable mercy is: it means "to vibrate to someone else's pain . . . and be moved to extravagant effort to alleviate that suffering."[48] Mercy in this sense does not simply *feel* compassion but moves beyond the feeling to "intentional kindness."[49] When Jesus looked at the crowds following him, he did not sigh or shoo them away even though it would have seemed completely reasonable to do so, but he had compassion on them and met their needs over and over, whether through teaching (Matthew 9:36), healing (14:14), or feeding (15:32). The merciful *see* people who hurt, and they take intentional steps toward loving those people and healing their pain, even if it means stepping into suffering themselves.

Jesus showed us that kind of risky love in his parable of the Good Samaritan in Luke 10:30–37. In this story, a Samaritan (an enemy of the Jews) gave a Jewish man medical care, transportation, housing, and a third of his week's salary to provide for him. He then promised to pay for any additional expenses the injured man would incur under the care of an innkeeper. We cannot calculate the "cost" of the inconvenience and the danger the Samaritan had already risked to care for him on the notorious Jericho road, but we know that he was willing to accept more intangible and tangible expense as well. Jesus told this story to show the connection between mercy and neighborly love, and we see in it that mercy is truly generous—it may even require you to give yourself away. Jesus "never meant to confirm my congenital preference for safe investments and limited liabilities."[50] On the contrary, he meant for you to take risks in mercy and so to practice real charity.

When you think about merciful living, how do you feel? Are you fearful because of the risks involved, because you already feel overwhelmed and think you cannot take on anything else, because you do not want your life overrun by needy people? Remember that charity always costs you something. We tend to think of charity as a privilege of the relatively wealthy who skim the top off their excess or relieve themselves of stuff they wanted once but now regard as junk—if I have extra, if that doesn't fit anymore, if that furniture has gone out of style, then people who cannot afford better will surely enjoy it. But practicing mercy hurt the Good Samaritan, and it hurt Jesus—it cost him his very life. It may also cost yours.

Remember all of the mercy that Jesus has shown you and how much that proves the Father's love for you. Does this not cause your fear to subside? Whatever you lose by showing mercy, you will gain back a hundredfold at the resurrection of the righteous (Luke 14:14). So do mercy. Moved by true compassion, those who have received mercy willingly practice charity.

In the Other Hand of Mercy, We Find Forgiveness

We must now take a step deeper, for mercy is much more than charity. The other side of mercy suspends justice and pays whatever debt is owed—again, at great cost to the one who shows the mercy. Tim Keller uses the word *absorb* to describe what happens in forgiveness—the one who forgives *absorbs* the debt owed. No debt ever evaporates into thin air. And when you pay the debt for the person who wronged you, that is forgiveness—absorbing the cost someone else owes.[51] Think about a towel that you use to wipe up a spill—if the towel does its job, the counter appears completely dry as though nothing ever happened. Mercy is like a towel that absorbs sin so completely, it's as though no one ever committed it.

Think about it another way. When someone borrows money from me, I expect to be paid back, so if the person never repays the debt, I will be reluctant to give when asked again by that person or anyone else. But to *absorb* the debt means never even keeping a record of what I am owed. When Peter wanted to put a limit on mercy by determining the point at which it was unreasonable to continue forgiving someone, Jesus told a parable in which he contrasted a king's amazing mercy against his servant's lack of mercy and claimed that we must forgive our brother countless times (Matthew 18:21–35). Those who have received mercy cannot afford to count the cost of forgiving others. No matter how often you are wronged, and no matter what the character of the person who wrongs you is like, Christians are obligated to keep on forgiving.

When we see that this is what Jesus intends for our forgiveness, most of us want to ask Peter's question in Matthew 18:21 again, just to make sure: "Wait. How often must I forgive my brother who sins against me? No more than seven times, right?" When we hear Jesus' response, we want to say, "Seventy-seven times? You're kidding! You cannot possibly mean this. Forgiveness cannot possibly be that lavish." Our hearts want to revolt against such reckless and incomprehensible forgiveness. It makes far more sense that those who wronged us should have to pay for what they have done; we should not have to forgive them, especially if they have come to us for forgiveness again and again. At this point, we start running through what Philip Yancey calls "the crystalline logic of unforgiveness."[52] See if this sounds familiar to you:

> He needs to learn a lesson. I don't want to encourage irresponsible behavior. I'll let her stew for a while; it will do her good. She needs to learn that actions have consequences. I was the wronged party—it's not up to me to make the first move. How can I forgive if he's not even sorry?[53]

We can come up with any number of good reasons to withhold forgiveness. We work hard to have Jesus' word to us in Matthew 18 die the death of a thousand qualifications. But Jesus allows no qualifications: "Whenever you stand praying, forgive, if you have *anything* against *anyone*" (Mark 11:25). Not, "If he really grovels, then forgive him" or "If you sense that she will be good from now on, then forgive her." Just, "Forgive."

Forgiveness never comes cheap, though. In a moral universe, our sins against each other cannot be ignored. Neither can our sins against God. That is why R. C. Sproul calls mercy *nonjustice*:

> Mercy is not justice, but it also is not injustice. Injustice violates righteousness. Mercy manifests kindness and grace and does no violence to righteousness. We may see *nonjustice* in God, which is mercy, but we never see *injustice* with God.[54]

And the *nonjustice* that God shows us in the gospel is only made possible because of the strict justice he showed his son on the cross.

At the cross, we see justice and mercy come together as God chooses to absorb the debt of sin we owe him. Through the gospel we enjoy the forgiveness of sins, not because God has pushed our sins aside but because he has absorbed their cost in his son. This is the only way that God can show the mercy of forgiveness to sinners. It allows him to be both "just and the justifier of the one who has faith in Jesus" (Romans 3:26).

Motivating Mercy

Those who have received God's mercy also practice mercy—it's like a natural byproduct. But that does not mean you simply become someone who forgives and shares. Mercy, as Jesus defines it, goes even deeper than genuine forgiveness and costly generosity to touch our *attitude* about and our *motivation* for mercy. You may, by your strong willpower or nice disposition or natural compassion, be merciful to some extent, but Jesus is not talking about temperament. The kind of mercy he refers to in this beatitude comes only through understanding the gospel of grace. You cannot earn a seat at the table of the gospel with your achievements, your pedigree, your record, or your personality. Rather, if you have a seat at the table, it is because you have been forgiven a debt you could never repay in a thousand lifetimes. You have been set free by God's forgiveness, and God's mercy has been poured out on you even though you deserved nothing but the strictest demands of justice. Knowing this fuels the Christian's mercy.

The king tells his slave in Matthew 18 that he should have forgiven the small debt he was owed because he knew the mercy of having been forgiven a large debt. So too, the Christian should show mercy because he has been forgiven a debt that far exceeds anything anyone else could owe him. Our hands are too occupied receiving God's forgiveness; we have no hand free with which to choke our neighbor or hold on to bitter roots against others. Christians therefore willingly give away their physical and financial resources—not to assuage their guilty consciences or earn points with their Creator, and certainly not to make themselves feel like great benefactors to the ignorant masses, but simply because they have received so much from God.

Is your heart enamored with its own generosity? Only the gospel can rescue you from such dangerous displays of mercy. Only the gospel will keep you humble enough to show mercy to others, because the gospel shows you that you are a debtor to mercy as well: "A sensitive social conscience and a life poured out in deeds of mercy to the needy is the inevitable sign of a person who has grasped the doctrine of God's grace."[55] So Christians are generous to all, but especially to the poor and needy, because Christ has been generous with them: "For you know the grace of our Lord Jesus Christ, that though he was rich, yet for your sake he became poor, so that you by his poverty might become rich" (2 Corinthians 8:9).

The Beatitudes have led us to this point: a merciful person knows that he is spiritually bankrupt before God, hates that his sin has broken God's heart by nailing his son to the cross, refuses to engage in self-protection, and longs for the only righteousness that will make him acceptable to God. The logic of the Beatitudes suggests that you cannot be merciful without those other attributes, but that with them, your mercy will never be reduced to a sense of superiority over the weak or a sense of smugness over the generosity of your heart. This holistic approach means that I, as a recipient of mercy, can see others with a sympathetic sorrow that moves me to action.[56] Only a heart responding to God's grace can produce this true mercy.

Grace or Works?

Turn your attention now to the final phrase in this beatitude: does Jesus say here that if you want God to be merciful to you, you had better be merciful to others? Does he say that if you want God's acceptance, you need to be a good, merciful person? Is he preaching salvation by philanthropy, salvation by forgiveness? Has he suddenly turned the tables on grace and shifted into salvation by works?

Imagine how hopeless we would all be if this were the case! If God's mercy toward me ultimately depends on how merciful I am to other people, then I am in big trouble. But the Beatitudes are not commands; they represent the profile of a Christian, the profile of someone who has already come to understand God's grace and is growing in that understanding. The Beatitudes are all about what happens to people when their hearts are gripped with the unmerited favor and undeserved acceptance of God. One attribute that naturally pours out of a heart like that is mercy.

So when it comes to mercy in the fifth beatitude, Jesus assumes that your mercy toward others is an infallible sign that you have *already* experienced the mercy of the gospel in your own life, which means you also look forward to experiencing more of God's mercy in the future. Jesus says that merciful people show by their attitudes and acts of mercy that God's mercy is upon them. Think of this beatitude, then, as one sure indicator that you have come to understand and are continuing to understand God's grace in the gospel. If you are growing in your practice of mercy, then you are growing in your understanding of the gospel of God's grace.

FOR YOUR HEAD

1. Do you earn God's mercy by being merciful? What does this beatitude assume about the merciful?
2. Discuss the material and immaterial sides of mercy.

FOR YOUR HEART

3. Describe a time when your mercy toward another person was a function of your sense of superiority rather than your confidence in Jesus' mercy for you.
4. How can reflecting on this beatitude help you show mercy to someone whom you are struggling to forgive right now? What does your struggle show that you fail to understand and believe about the mercy of God?

FOR YOUR CHURCH

5. How would you amend the counsel you have given to another believer who has struggled to forgive someone? What counsel would you find helpful?
6. Showing mercy can (and often should) involve more than writing a check to the needy or the organizations that support them. What are some needs in your church that God may be calling you to take risks to meet?

FOR YOUR CITY

7. How does this beatitude mobilize you toward ministries of mercy for the people in your city?
8. What can you do right now in your non-Christian social orbit to demonstrate the mercy of the gospel through your deeds?

7

THE GOOD NEWS THAT MAKES YOU HONEST

How clever you are, my dear! You never mean a single
word you say.
> — Lady Huntstanton in Oscar Wilde's
> *A Lady of No Importance*

Blessed are the pure in heart, for they shall see God.
> — Matthew 5:8

Hypocrisy is a great enemy of the Christian faith—maybe the *greatest* enemy of the Christian faith. Christians all struggle with inauthenticity, believing one thing and doing another, and while we do not like confessing this to fellow believers, we seem to have particular trouble being honest with unbelievers, trying to act more moral than we really are. We talk big but seem blind, or else like liars, since others plainly see our inconsistences even as we continue to insist that Christians always have everything together. Because of this, hypocrisy sits on top of the list of outsiders' objections to Christianity: "I can't stand Christians. They're all a bunch of hypocrites."

How do you respond to this objection? When your unbelieving friends and family point out hypocrisy in the church or even in your own life, what do you say? Perhaps you say something like, "You can't judge Christianity by Christians; you have to look to Jesus." There is some truth to that, after all. To assess the Christian faith itself, you need to look at the Bible and take your cues from Jesus. But that statement can also be a copout because Christians themselves still belong in the equation. What others see in you matters.

Throughout the New Testament, we are told to live in a way that will make our non-Christian friends sit up and take notice and learn what the Christian faith is all about (see Colossians 4:5–6 and 1 Peter 3:15). There is, then, a very real sense in which our unbelieving friends are absolutely right to judge Christianity by the way we live. If the lives of so-called Christians are generally characterized by hypocrisy, then we essentially declare to the world that Christianity is a false and powerless religious system. We might as well tell the naysayers they are right: "Yes, we are hypocrites. Too bad Christianity can't fix us." Or, worse: "You're right. And Jesus is fine with that."

We need to point others to Jesus with our words *and* with our lives. Jesus has not failed: he has overthrown hypocrisy and will not leave us to drown in a sea of our own duplicity. In fact, he tells us that the sign of genuine Christianity is the absence of hypocrisy because he has put to death all of your excuses for insincerity and presumptuousness. He calls purity of heart an essential component of the profile of the true Christian—along with poverty of spirit, mourning over our sin, meekness, hungering and thirsting for righteousness, mercy, peacemaking, and persecution—because those who understand God's grace enjoy purity of heart as a way of life.

Good, Nice People

Jesus says that only the pure in heart will see God—not the civil people, the "good" people, or the nice people. Don't let the outside fool you. The moralist may not commit egregious, flagrant, blatant, overt, loud sins, and he may think he is faithful simply because he avoids the big ones. But God pays attention to the sins of his heart.

If the religious moralist does not receive what he wants God to give him for how "faithful" he has been to God, he will be angry with God and may eventually find himself committing the very sins he so loudly denounced—sins he at one point in his life thought himself incapable of. He practices a particular brand of hypocrisy, then, because he believes God is who he says he is only so long as that works for him personally. So do not think that Jesus is talking about cleaning up your life. A person can have a very clean life and simultaneously harbor "a secret antipathy to . . . God,"[57] a deep-seated hatred for God that may only emerge when things do not go his way.

Maybe you read that and think, "I'm not like that. I may not be perfect, but I don't have some secret hatred for God. I'm a nice guy!" Perhaps so, but the Bible frequently calls into question the "nice guys" because they have become deceived by their very niceness, so we would be wise to interrogate ourselves often and seek renewal rather than maintain goodness. In his classic *Mere Christianity*, C. S. Lewis wrote about this very phenomenon in a chapter called, "Nice People or New Men," which argues that the Christian faith is not about making people *nice* but about making people *new*:

> A world of nice people, content in their own niceness, looking no further, turned away from God, would be just as desperately in need of salvation as a miserable world – and might even be more difficult to save.
>
> For mere improvement is not redemption, though redemption always improves people in the here and now and will, in the end, improve them to a degree we cannot yet imagine. God became man to turn creatures into sons: not simply to produce better men of the old kind but to produce a new kind of man. It is not like teaching a horse to jump better and better, but like turning a horse into a winged creature.[58]

This is what happens when you become a Christian—you do not go to reform school, nor do you simply become a better or nicer person. Rather, you become a completely *new* person—like a workhorse transforming not into Seabiscuit, as amazing a racehorse as he was, but into Pegasus and flying across the ancient Greek sky.

A Heart Condition

To suggest that you need to become a winged creature rather than simply a cooler horse implies that there is something wrong with your horse-ness in the first place. If we could get on fine by just improving the old hearts, we would, but we cannot—there is something fundamentally wrong with the very essence of who we are. Jesus says that only the pure in heart see God, which assumes that we do not all have pure hearts and that we do not all see God. Rather, we all have a terrible heart condition: our hearts are not *whole*, much less are our *whole hearts* oriented to God.

In the Bible, the *heart* does not refer simply to the emotions, though that is how we typically use the word in English. If we say someone's heart is broken, we mean that he is sad. If someone's heart is full, she *feels* happy or satisfied. But a biblical understanding of the heart involves the emotions, the intellect, and the will. Your heart emotes, thinks, and desires. It is your root, the seat of your true self, your "psyche at the deepest level"[59]—the place from which your thoughts, feelings, and actions flow.[60] Your *heart* signifies what you are all about at the center of your being; it is your true identity.

It should seem obvious, then, that Christianity is a faith of the heart; it is not primarily about compliance with certain rules and regulations, living a certain lifestyle, or conforming to moral and ethical norms. Christianity is not about your behavior . . . but this does not mean that your behavior means nothing. To the contrary, Jesus says that what you do with hands and mouth actually expresses your heart (Luke 6:45). This means that if you deal only with what happens on the outside, you fall into the ditch of hypocrisy, becoming a whitewashed tomb—clean on the outside, but full of filth on the inside. You can assess what is going on in your heart by what you say and do, but if you clean up your behavior only, you will miss the mark wide. The fundamental issue for the Christian faith is what goes on *in* your heart.

You may be worried right now. If you have as much trouble as I do *acting* pure, how can you ever hope to *be* pure in heart? That means a heart that is clean, unmixed, "unalloyed, unadulterated,"[61] complete, not duplicitous—a heart that makes your whole being have integrity. A pure heart frees you from "the tyranny of a divided self,"[62] making your inner life whole, and your whole life oriented in a single direction—toward God. So Jesus reaches far with this phrase, suggesting that Christianity is about the transformation of your entire inner life, the metamorphosis of your whole psychology from something fragmented into something cohesive.

How does this happen? The gospel moves to the deepest recesses of your being and messes around with how you tick, renewing you from the inside out. Our hearts need renovation that only Jesus can do. Our hearts need cleansing because they are sick with sin.

When we talk about sin, we most often mean our various wrong acts or even desires, but we must consider here the sin beneath the sin—the general condition of sin that gives birth to all particular sins. Sin has various effects on the motives and intentions of our hearts, and that kind of sin must get cleaned out in order for a heart to become pure. This is why we know that purity of heart cannot be a temperament or a personality trait; that which makes our hearts sick with sin is the sin at the root of our humanity. We all by nature have impure hearts—not even the person you consider so sweet and pure has a heart left unscathed by the ravages of our fall into sin.

How do I know that we *all* have impure, sinful hearts? Jesus answers that question: "For out of the heart come evil thoughts, murders, adulteries, fornications, thefts, false witness, slanders. These are the things which defile the man; but to eat with unwashed hands does not defile the man" (Matthew 15:19–20 NASB). All sin has its root in the heart, from which we act and speak (see Matthew 12:34). If filthy things come flying out of your mouth, then there are all kinds of filthy things inside your heart. Those words do not come from nowhere; they come from an idolatrous heart.

Personal Loyalty and Idolatry of the Heart

Throughout the Old Testament, when God speaks of purifying the heart, he means that we need our hearts cleansed from idolatry. Consider Ezekiel 36:25 NASB in which God makes a promise: "Then I will sprinkle clean water on you, and you will be clean; I will cleanse you *from all your filthiness and from all your idols.*" Do you think that you need cleansing from idolatry? You probably do not have a statue glued to your dashboard or a totem pole on your front lawn. You probably do not prepare sacrifices for the god of the sun or the god of the earth or the god of the McDonald's drive-thru or whatever god you might think of. You may even be atheist or agnostic. How can you be an idolater if you are at least skeptical as to whether there is such a thing as the divine, however conceived?

From the perspective of the Bible, an idol is anything you live for other than the true and living God—the Christian God. Whatever you orient your life around, whatever lights you up, whatever you are ten-fingers-and-ten-toes committed to, whatever you value most in the universe—that's the object of your worship. "Okay, then, like what?" you might ask. There is an almost limitless number of idols for you to choose from, and all of them have adverse consequences for your life—idols of comfort, praise, security, affirmation, approval, personal reputation—you name it. Psalm 115:4–8 puts it like this:

> Their idols are silver and gold,
> the work of human hands.
> They have mouths, but do not speak;
> eyes, but do not see.
> They have ears, but do not hear;
> noses, but do not smell.
> They have hands, but do not feel;
> feet, but they do not walk;
> and they do not make a sound in their throat.
> *Those who make them will become like them;*
> so do all who trust in them.

Your idols eat you up. They promise the world and give you only heartache. Every sin resident in our hearts will spew out of our mouths and into our behaviors because our hearts are fountains flowing with the water of disloyalty to God. A pure-hearted person recognizes this and responds to God's cordial demand to be the center of his life by discovering and ditching his idols, chopping them down and burning them to powder. This will take time and energy, and it will hurt, but it is worth it because purity of heart has to do with our singleness of devotion to God, faithfulness to God, "undivided loyalty"[63] to God. First and foremost, then, purity of heart involves personal loyalty to God. But it also has immediate outward effects.

Relational Honesty

What begins as personal loyalty to God will work itself out in personal relationships: purity of heart primarily describes our posture to God, but that posture affects the way we interact with other people as well. This is why Jesus told us to love others sacrificially at the same time that he told us to love God supremely: "You shall love the Lord your God with all your heart and with all your soul and with all your mind. This is the great and first commandment. And a second is like it: You shall love your neighbor as yourself" (Matthew 22:37–39). Thus, we see purity of heart worked out in human relationships where my "whole life, public and private, is transparent before God *and men*."[64] My heart needs not only loyalty to God, but also honesty with other people—"a lack of duplicity, singleness of intention"[65] in the way we relate to one another.

Bottom line, Christians are not fake. We must instead be honest—honest with other people about our struggles, our sins, our weaknesses, our flaws, and the mistakes we have made. We should not pretend to be anything better than we really are, though we do that nearly constantly: "We are tempted to wear a different mask and play a different role according to each occasion."[66] Ask yourself, then: does anyone know the real you? Do you ever take off your mask before others? How about the pious mask that you wear with church friends? Do those outside of the church ever see you depending on God's grace or do you appear to think that you have "arrived" at some spiritual high point?

Do not think, after all, that purity of heart means having a perfect or sinless heart. If that is what you think, then you do not yet understand what Jesus is talking about. This beatitude is another great irony of the Christian faith: a person who has purity of heart acknowledges before God and other people that he is not yet fully pure in heart. Hypocrites refuse to admit this. They lie to God, to themselves, and to other people by suggesting that they are something they are not, that they are better than they really are, that they do not currently or desperately need the Savior who speaks and embodies the Beatitudes, that they do not themselves need rescue.

But to be pure in heart means you have the courage to admit to God and yourself and other people that you are as bad as you really are, that your heart really is impure, that you need continual cleansing from the Lord. In this sense, a pure heart is suspicious of itself even while it acts generously toward other people. Like Thomas Watson said, "The hypocrite suspects others and has charitable thoughts of himself. The sincere Christian has charitable thoughts of others and suspects himself."[67] The pure-hearted person always holds out hope for others because he knows how much he himself needs hope.

For this reason also, pure-hearted people have the freedom to be brutally honest with others about themselves—open and honest and transparent about how deep their need still is and about how much cleansing they still require. In public and private, before God and other people, the pure in heart are honest. They are the same in their prayer room as they are in their living room. This is purity of heart.

The True Threat

In a post-Christian culture like ours where many regard moderate religiosity as a good thing, the danger for the church is to reduce the Christian faith to a lifestyle—a subculture complete with its own music and literature and fashions and jargon. This is especially dangerous for those who grow up in the church. Christian parents sometimes worry about their kids being influenced by worldly evils in our oversexed, violent, materialistic culture. They worry that their kids will be negatively influenced by the literature they read, the movies and television shows they watch, the video games they play, and the music they listen to.

Although these things are certainly not benign and do have the capacity to negatively influence children, they are not half as danger-ous as reducing Christianity to moralistic religion. These kinds of

Christian parents focus on relatively small matters and ignore the possibility of a much more terrible reality. Because it seems so likely that our churched children and teens would remain loyal to the church all their days and live very moral lives, we tend not to worry about them, but their very religiosity makes them even more susceptible to get crushed by the hurricanes of their own sin and the schemes of Satan than a bare house in the path of a Category 5 hurricane.

Consider how people typically prepare for natural disaster. If you live in New Orleans or the Florida Keys, you probably have some plywood and nails and a hammer on hand to board up your windows and doors when hurricanes come. But we don't do that in Minnesota: there is no threat of hurricane here. That's because people prepare for what seems plausible, but not for extremely unlikely scenarios. Churched children raised by deeply committed Christian parents are not as likely to end up practicing Wicca as they are to serve faithfully but numbly in a local church. For if churched children remain unaffected by and inoculated to the gospel—wholesale consumers of just enough gospel lingo and institutional Christianity to look the part—they will completely miss the heart of Christianity. They will miss out on purity of heart.

Not a Matter of Religion But of Seeing God

Some think that only religious people can be hypocrites, and if we defined hypocrisy simply as holier-than-thou, smug moralizing, that would make sense. But the fact of the matter is that hypocrisy goes much deeper than self-righteous religious fanaticism. Hypocrisy is the sin of lying to God, yourself, and other people about who you really are on the inside, so whether you are religious is irrelevant. A God-denying, God-hating, God-rejecting atheist can still be a hypocrite. In fact, that sort of person is the worst kind of hypocrite because he lies to himself about God being there. At least the religious hypocrite doesn't lie about that . . . or does he? Oh, he might not be an *actual* atheist, but he is a *practical* one because he lives his life as if God does not see his heart. Psalm 14:1 says, "The fool says in his heart, 'There is no God,'" and that is not a word to atheists, but to the people of God.

We all, at one level or another, lie to God—either by explicitly claiming that he is not there or else by living our lives *as if* he is not there. Hypocrisy, then, is not so much the opposite of sincerity as the opposite of honesty. Purity of heart may seem like a lofty goal, but only when you think of it as a product; instead, think of it as living authentically by grace. The pure in heart live courageously and vulnerably in the presence of the true and living God. They are fiercely loyal to him, and they alone enjoy the blessing of seeing him.

What is so great about seeing God? It is only the capstone of human existence. To see God means to know him intimately, to be "admitted to his presence" and "awestruck by his glory" and "comforted by his grace."[68] We were made for that. Indeed, being with God is the reason we exist: "You and I are meant for the audience chamber of God; you and I are being prepared to enter into the presence of the King of kings."[69] In the Bible, there is nothing better than seeing the Lord. Every other blessing we might enjoy in this life—family, friends, food, excitement, beautiful destinations, natural wonders, music, art, baseball, the smell of a fire on a cold night, the birth of a child, sex—whatever you enjoy in this life (as truly wonderful as it may be) is simply a reflection of the glory of God. Jonathan Edwards, that great eighteenth century American theologian, reflecting on the glories of heaven, put it like this:

> When a saint dies, he has no cause at all to grieve because he leaves his friends and relations whom he dearly loves; for he doth not properly leave them, he enjoys them still in Christ, because every thing that they love in them, and love them for, is in Christ in an infinite degree, whether it be nearness of relation, or any perfection and good received, or love in us, or a likeness in dispositions, or whatever is a rational ground of love.[70]

As we await that eternal future, we live in the present age and see God most clearly in the gospel of Jesus Christ. Through the gospel, God sheds light on dark hearts so that they might see God

(2 Corinthians 4:4–6). And this means that to whatever degree we lack purity of heart, to that degree have we failed to comprehend the gospel. That is, the reason why we do not enjoy purity of heart now is actually that we have not seen God fully in the gospel. This is a Christian paradox: until we see God, we cannot be truly pure in heart, and until we are pure in heart, we cannot see God. It sounds like a catch-22, but it is not. God unveils himself in the gospel, and seeing him as he is will make us fiercely loyal and brutally honest. By seeing in the gospel what Jesus has done for me, I cannot help but feel loyal to him, endeared to him, and therefore gladly vulnerable before him and before others who belong to him.

In the gospel, I see Jesus dying on the cross for me, showing true fidelity to me despite my near-constant infidelity, and I am compelled to love God with unwavering loyalty and live in relational honesty. The gospel shows me that I am a vile, pretentious hypocrite—a person that Jesus had to die for. And if the person whose opinion means the most to me in the world has accepted me with a comprehensive knowledge of my impurity, no one else's opinion of me will make or break my existence. I am free to admit my failures to myself and to others because I no longer fear rejection.[71] Why would I care what the other serfs think about me? I am in full view of the king of the universe—and he smiles at me because of his son. I am in full view of the king of the universe, gazing upon him in all his glory, and I live to tell the tale. Seeing God is the gospel.

Look at Me

When your non-Christian friends now accuse you of hypocrisy, will you say, "Don't look at me; look at Jesus"? You should certainly point them to Jesus, but you might also tell them something about how purity of heart is not about moral perfection but about honesty before God and others. You might begin by sharing that you have acknowledged and ditched your idols as the sum total of your existence. There is a new king on the throne of your heart—the true and living God—the Lord Jesus Christ. From there, you might share how imperfect you have been in your faithfulness to the new God of your life, yet how faithful he has remained in the project of making you completely new in the image of Christ.

Then, you can say, "Look at me. This is what the Christian life is all about. It's not about me and my achievements and my ability to be good; it's about Jesus Christ and all he has done for me through the gospel. It's about the fact that I, like you, needed a Savior—someone to purify me from my idols, to take the reins of my life, and to cause me to see God. And Christianity is about the fact that I'm *still* like you in a very big way—I still need that Savior." The pure in heart see God and know how infinitely more pure he is, so they gaze upon him in his beauty and long to see him better forever.

FOR YOUR HEAD

1. How is purity of heart different from perfection of heart?
2. What does it mean to see God?

FOR YOUR HEART

3. Purity of heart before God leads to purity of heart with other people. Explain why your relationship to God parallels your relationships with people.
4. Name some idols of your heart that you are currently having a hard time dethroning (for example, idols of comfort, acclaim, peace, appreciation, security). Why do you want to hold onto those idols?

FOR YOUR CHURCH

5. Share with a Christian friend some way in which you have seen him or her grow in purity of heart over the last six months. Take a moment to thank God for the fruit you have seen.
6. What is the number one obstacle keeping you from being honest with other Christians? (Do not give the "right" answer, but the honest one.)

FOR YOUR CITY

7. Perhaps the greatest complaint against Christians marshaled by non-Christians is our hypocrisy. How does this beatitude

shape future interactions with them such that you legitimately weaken their complaint?

8. Take a moment to brainstorm what would happen in your community if it experienced the truth of this beatitude. Now pray it into reality.

8

THE GOOD NEWS THAT WAGES PEACE

All we are saying is give peace a chance.

— John Lennon

Blessed are the peacemakers, for they shall be called sons of God.

— Matthew 5:9

You can take a public poll about peace just by observing bumper stickers: from "Wage Peace" to "Peace the Old-Fashioned Way" in which a B-52 makes the peace symbol to "Visualize Peace" to "coexist" with the letters formed by different religious symbols, the stickers on our cars preach our politics of peace. One morning, I pulled out of a Starbucks' parking lot and noticed a Volkswagen Bug wearing a bumper sticker with "Blessed are the peacemakers" on it, and I had to wonder if the driver had any clue about what Jesus meant when he said that. We live in a world full of war and insurgencies and uprisings and conflicts, and everyone from beauty queens to drivers of cute cars seems to long for peace among individuals, communities, and governments.

Of course, there are obvious exceptions—namely, those instigating and sustaining the quarrels and conflicts in families, churches, schools, businesses, and nations. If *everyone* were interested in peace, we would take more initiative to put down our weapons (physical and metaphorical) and work toward solving our problems, wouldn't we? But even the most gentle among us get riled up at *something*, whether small offenses in the grocery store or global problems that threaten the safety of innocent civilians. Justice and peace seem always at odds with each other, and solutions appear complex at best. We slap bumper stickers on our cars as a signal to others that they should at least quit bothering us and try to do right.

Some people think we would all be better off if no one ever made a fuss—if everyone just chilled out and only as a last resort scheduled nonviolent sit-ins. Others think the solution is in blowing our enemies to bits and turning their countries into parking lots. But both ways assume that we achieve peace through our own efforts: "I am so quiet and calm that no one would ever fight with me" or "Nobody messes with the country with the biggest nuclear weapons."

By this point in our study of the Beatitudes, you will not be surprised to learn that Jesus has something radically different in mind when he calls peacemakers blessed. Jesus made peace, but not through mousiness *or* braggadocio, and those with whom he makes peace do the same work through the power of the gospel. We may start out as wallflowers or warmongers, but those whom Jesus makes his brothers and sisters become like their elder brother. They bear up and stand down.

War! What Is It Good For?

Many ancient Jews thought they needed to make peace through war, and many of the people following Jesus expected him to lead the charge. They knew that placidly "taking it" did not work, so armed revolt seemed like the only way to eliminate wickedness and oppression. In fact, many anticipated that ultimate peace for God's people would come through a great war between Jews and Gentiles at the end of the world, and the Jews wanted that to happen soon. When you have been oppressed, marginalized, maligned, and treated with contempt, your religious sensibilities constantly trampled upon, your ability to govern hamstrung by political thugs and Jewish collaborators, your money virtually stolen from you through an unjust system of tax farming, you too might start to think that you have no choice but to get out the bricks and baseball bats and do some damage. It is no wonder the Jews of Jesus' day hoped in war.

Still today, fighting often seems like the fast track to fulfilling our individual and national desires, and it does work sometimes—at least for those who are bigger than their opponents. We want what we want, and we will commit violence against others and heart-adultery against God to get it (see James 4:1–6). When other people or institutions or nations become obstacles to my getting what I want, what I live for, what I long for other than the Lord, I fight. Yet history has proven that when people wage war to achieve peace and justice, even the best results suffer from profound brokenness, including physical destruction and bitter hearts.

In the end, conflict usually keeps even the instigators from getting what they want. The battle escalates to the point that we forget why we started fighting in the first place. All that remains is our pride, the need to save face, to make a point, to put the opponents in their place, to teach someone a lesson. It is easy to embrace a superficial understanding of peace, but ceasing to fight rarely means that we made peace or even ceased to want war.

We like to think that we can do good on our own. We definitely do not want to admit that if we will have peace in our hearts and in our world, God must do it, but that is exactly what the peacemaker knows and says over and over. Those whom God reconciled to himself have now received "the ministry of reconciliation" (2 Corinthians 5:18), which means God himself has equipped them to do his very work in the world. Peacemakers labor as "ambassadors for Christ" (5:20), imploring others to be at peace with God. And that labor is a grace-filled miracle, for how can anyone who is naturally oriented to self-reliance and self-determination actually admit that he is desperate for God apart from God's own work of grace in his heart?

So it is one thing to talk about peace; it is quite another to *make* it. Unlike being a peace-lover or even a peacekeeper, being a peace-*maker* means doing nearly impossible, bothersome work[72] at great risk to yourself. If you undertake this kind of painstaking, pride-swallowing, and dangerous labor, you run the risk of being misunderstood, maligned, and even made into the enemy by those you are trying to reconcile. Nevertheless, the peacemaker has a "spirit . . . that delights to pour oil upon the troubled waters, that aims to right wrongs, that seeks to restore kindly relations by dealing with and removing difficulties and by neutralizing and silencing acrimonies."[73] The peacemaker considers it a pleasure to do one of the hardest jobs in the world.

Working Hard at Making Peace

Have you ever tried to get in the middle of two people at odds with each other? Forget churches and schools and families and nations for a moment and consider how hard it is to help two warring individuals come to peace with one another. At times during my pastoral ministry, married couples in deeply troubled waters have sought me out for counsel, appearing to desire reconciliation to one another, but sometimes the husband and wife are so fortified in their own positions as to be utterly immoveable in the direction of reconciliation. I have even experienced situations in which all my efforts to help the couple have been used against me, such that they finally blame me as the reason for their troubles. I have certainly seen some counseling sessions get ugly.

Peacemakers should expect these kinds of reactions to their work. We sometimes think of peacemakers as people who do not create waves, who avoid strife, who put up with chaos and schism—as though peacemaking is primarily about avoiding conflict.[74] Instead, what peacemakers do is seek opportunities to actively help institutions and individuals reconcile for the common good. Frankly, that reality makes the bumper stickers celebrating peace seem impractical and trite.

We all love the idea of ending wars, seeing happy families, and embracing racial reconciliation in our cities, but peacemakers get their hands dirty and partner with the Holy Spirit in the work of reconciliation. They put all their poverty of spirit, mourning, meekness, hunger and thirst, mercy, and purity to work, and they literally *make* peace. Thus, the cohesiveness of the Beatitudes teaches us that peacemakers are more than just peacemakers. To be a true peacemaker, you must have the complete profile of the Christian—you must embody all of the Beatitudes.

Peacemakers are not proud but poor in spirit: they recognize their own incompetence and gladly depend upon God for everything. Peacemakers are not cold to their own sin: they are keenly aware of how destitute and broken sin has made us. Peacemakers do not see themselves as better than anyone else: they are meek. Peacemakers have abandoned their own pursuit of righteousness: they hunger and thirst for the righteousness of Jesus. Peacemakers forgive guilty people and act on the pity they feel for broken people: they get into the messiness of the world because of God's great mercy in the gospel. And peacemakers have pure hearts: they are loyal to God and honest with others. Peacemakers make peace because they know real and full blessedness from God. Peacemakers do the hard work of reconciliation because they themselves have been reconciled to God.

Peacemaking and Evangelism

Peacemakers know how blessed they are, and they express their happiness this way: they love to announce the good news that peace comes when God rules (Isaiah 52:7). Peacemakers declare the good news of what God has done in Jesus Christ, not simply reconciling warring individuals and institutions with one another, but fundamentally reconciling sinners to God. Of course, this means that peacemakers must let others in on a troublesome fact that they might not realize—that they are at war with their maker. True peacemaking may start a few fights before it brings any calm or quiet.

Are you willing to admit that people are hostile toward God and even at war with him? Colossians 1:21 describes our natural state as "alienated and hostile in mind, doing evil deeds," and Romans 8:7 says the natural mind "is hostile to God, for it does not submit to God's law; indeed, it cannot." But the fact of the matter is that few people actually see themselves as hostile toward God. We might see ourselves as not really into God, or not all that religious, but we do not typically see ourselves as actively warring with God.

Think about how you respond to things that directly affect your life but that are clearly out of your control. At every natural disaster, even people who do not normally think much about God tend to ask, "Where is God in this?" And if you are a religious person, you will get angry with God if he does not "come through" for you on something you really want—like a healthy child or a healed spouse, getting into your top school or landing that dream job, closing on a new house or making your kids obedient. Most enmity to God sleeps quietly until things do not go well.

So peacemakers must begin by helping people acknowledge their hostility toward God. They move behind enemy lines to tell people who are perfectly content to remain indifferent toward God that they are actually at war. They must then communicate that God will put his gun down if you unconditionally surrender to his cordial demand that you submit your life to his rule. This message will not sit very well with most people. Once you set out on your peacemaking mission to the world, you must prepare to take it on the chin.

You will be persecuted for your faith, especially when you have the audacity to suggest that there is such a thing as truth, that this truth is found only in Jesus, and that all people should yield to the authority of Jesus as king and sole Savior. If you tell people that the war between them and God is serious and that the only way it can end is if they embrace the gospel, you will get kicked in the teeth. And you will take a special beating if you have the audacity to preach that gospel to people who say they are Christians, inviting them to question whether they genuinely belong to God. It is dangerous to tell professed Christians that if they do not see themselves in all of the Beatitudes, then they have not yet understood the grace of God. It is dangerous to tell people that all their years of so-called service in the church and the community may be nothing but a rickety, dry, rotten wooden bridge of their own righteousness suspended over the burning flames of hell. Jesus was persecuted for saying that, and the original twelve disciples were too; so will you be persecuted if you continue to produce the evidence of encountering God's grace through Jesus Christ.

Nevertheless, peacemakers are evangelists because they cannot help but share the good news of Jesus with their families and friends and colleagues and classmates. They care about the spiritual condition of others, and they do not want them to be at war with God anymore. At times, this means speaking directly, and at other times, this means speaking rather gently. Peacemakers are not belligerent or obnoxious, but they are not cowards either. Peacemakers right wrongs and restore kind relations between individuals and institutions, preaching the gospel to enemies of God.

Peacemaking and Adoption

A person who has yet to understand God's grace might not think peacemaking is all that great of a job, but once you have received the gift of peace with him, then the effort of making peace elsewhere seems glorious and worth the effort. That is because you know that the real blessing of peacemaking is not actually the peace you achieve but the extreme intimacy of relationship you enjoy with God.[75] God does not just tolerate us; he proactively loves us, having picked us and made us permanently his children through adoption.

Think about the kind of kids the Lord adopts: every sinner that he makes into a son started out as a rebellious, disobedient, selfish, indignant brat. Not only did we not deserve our adoption, we fought against it kicking and screaming! Yet we will never be disowned; our status as God's kids can never change. Nothing "will be able to separate us from the love of God in Christ Jesus our Lord" (Romans 8:39) because his love for us is nothing less than the love of adoption (Romans 8:15–17). The Father let you murder his only begotten Son in order to adopt you as his son or daughter through faith in Christ. Because of what Jesus has done, you can be God's beloved child. And you can be confident that since you did not deserve his love in the first place, he will never remove it based on your performance. You did not earn adoption but received it as a gift without any reference to your own goodness, so you can be sure that he will not take it away when you fail him now. Nothing can separate you from the adoptive love of God that is in Christ Jesus.

If you have the privilege of belonging to God through adoption, would you not also embrace the privilege of living like a child of God? When you do the work of peacemaking, you get to emulate the Father you love and take part in his character.[76] You get to be like your dad. In this beatitude, Jesus says something profound about our heavenly Father's character: by connecting the work of peacemaking to our sonship, Jesus tells us that one of God's main characteristics is peacemaking. Indeed, God is the ultimate peacemaker, "making peace by the blood of his cross" (Colossians 1:20).

You cannot make yourself a peacemaker any more than you can make yourself a child of God. Being a peacemaker means first that you must come to know God's peace through the blood of Jesus on the cross. And to continue the work of sonly peacemaking requires continually doing the same thing: look to the peace-giving, adoption-securing blood of Jesus on the cross. When you see Jesus dying because of your hostility to God and loving you so much that he would die *in order to* reconcile you to God, you will find yourself more and more compelled to be a peacemaker yourself. You will also want others to know the liberty, joy, and security of peace with God that comes with the permanent blessing of being called children of God.

Ask yourself whether you are a peacemaker. Look at your life and assess whether you know the blessing and the privilege and the responsibility of God's adoption. If not, run to the blood of the cross by which the Father reconciles all things to himself, thus establishing peace—the peace we all so desperately need. And then get to work. Your heavenly Father is doing the work of peace, and he invites you to do this kingdom work with him.

FOR YOUR HEAD

1. Why is our sonship integral to being peacemakers?

2. How is God the Father the ultimate peacemaker?
3. What makes peacemaking such painstaking work?

FOR YOUR HEART

4. James 4:1 says, "What causes quarrels and what causes fights among you? Is it not this, that your passions are at war within you?" Then in verse 4, we are called "adulteress people." This means that all our hostility toward others is rooted in our idolatry—spiritual adultery committed by loving other things rather than or more than God. What idols are blocking God's peace in your life right now?
5. When you forget your adoption, how do you tend to behave?
6. How does knowing that you're a permanent member of God's family lead you to peacemaking?

FOR YOUR CHURCH

7. Where is God calling you to act as a peacemaker in your local church? What insights from this chapter will equip you for that work?
8. Church splits are some of the most heart-wrenching events in the life of the local church. What can you do to prevent these from happening? How can you be a *preventative* peacemaker?

FOR YOUR CITY

9. The most fundamental enmity that exists in the world is the enmity between God and human beings. Thus, the work of peacemaking is fundamentally evangelistic. Take a moment to write down the names of three people in your social orbit. Pray for open doors of opportunity to be a peacemaker in their lives this week.

9

THE GOOD NEWS THAT GETS YOU PUNCHED IN THE FACE

Well, here's another nice mess you've gotten me into!
— Oliver Hardy, *Sons of the Desert*

Blessed are those who are persecuted for righteousness' sake, for theirs is the kingdom of heaven. Blessed are you when others revile you and persecute you and utter all kinds of evil against you falsely on my account. Rejoice and be glad, for your reward is great in heaven, for so they persecuted the prophets who were before you.
— Matthew 5:10–12

Throughout the Beatitudes, Jesus delivers blow after blow to moralism, saying you do not have what it takes, nor can you muster up what it takes, to be blessed. Now we see his final blow, and it may be the strangest yet, for here he says that the really enviable people in the world—those who know objectively happy circumstances—are those persecuted for the sake of righteousness. This takes the cake.

Persecution comes in various forms, including systematic and programmatic oppression, unjust harassment, verbal and physical abuse, misunderstanding, mistreatment, and even murder . . . and it could never match anyone's definition of happiness. Jesus has made odd claims in the Beatitudes, but who could have predicted this one? Certainly no one in his original audience.

Unlike most of the previous beatitudes, there is no precedent for this claim in the Old Testament.[77] On the contrary, the Jewish Scriptures suggest that persecuted people *cannot* be blessed by virtue of their persecution: the two categories are mutually exclusive. Nevertheless, Jesus not only calls persecuted people blessed but claims that persecution is an essential component of life as a Christian. Why? Simply put, those who have been and continue to be persecuted are blessed because they possess the kingdom of heaven. These people have completely let go of whatever personal moral achievements they could have put on their spiritual résumés and have received the yoke of Jesus instead, so they have received a much greater reward. Those who have taken up persecution as their past and present and future reality know for sure that they belong to God.

Riled Up for All the Wrong Reasons

Note at the outset that Jesus does not simply call persecuted people blessed. Rather, he pronounces God's blessing on people who have been persecuted for the sake of *righteousness*. There are many reasons why people who dislike your Christianity might persecute you, but your Christianity may have nothing to do with it. Think about how Peter distinguishes between suffering as a Christian (1 Peter 4:15–16) and suffering when you did wrong (2:19–20). You might take a beating because you are an obnoxious, belligerent, sinful, self-righteous prig, but that is not blessed—your own sin brought about that suffering.

Unfortunately, this kind of suffering seems all too common for Christians. We chalk up all dislike others might feel toward us as "persecution for righteousness' sake" when it may be nothing of the sort. Instead of manifesting hearts of humility and mourning and meekness (the first three beatitudes), we walk around with chips on our shoulders. We act as if some vast conspiracy is brewing in America over the Christian faith, with naysayers organized and arrayed against us. We feel like we live life on the cultural margins, so we take that as our identity: we count our marginalization as our righteousness. And when you stop looking to Jesus as your only righteousness, things invariably turn ugly. Rather than acting on principle, you start acting from prejudice;[78] you assume that everyone hates you, and you act in a way that confirms it. Now you will definitely be persecuted, but not for the sake of righteousness—for the sake of self-righteousness.

Do you see the irony? When you justify your existence with the fact that you belong to an oppressed minority in an increasingly secularized culture, you will be persecuted, and that will only sink you more firmly into your identity as a victim. But this is not blessed persecution—it is unnecessary, silly, foolish punishment that you only brought on yourself by defining your identity by your own righteousness. Experiencing trouble that you deserve is not persecution; you have brought that upon yourself by being obnoxious. Rather, by definition, "persecution" is *unjust* harassment, physical violence, and verbal abuse. And Jesus says that persecution is a sure sign that you have come to understand the Christian faith.

Righteousness That Offends

In this beatitude, Jesus offers two reasons for blessed persecution—righteousness (verse 10) and Jesus (verse 11)—but they are really the same thing. Christians have received Jesus' comprehensively perfect righteousness as a gift, and as a result, we actually become more and more like Jesus himself. The righteousness that Jesus says people will hate is the righteousness that you begin to possess as you grow in your understanding of what Jesus has done for you. It is the righteousness that you practice simply by obeying the gospel. The seed of Jesus' righteousness bears fruit in those who believe, and their Christlike lives attract hostility. Nobody minds if you try to be a good person, but if you receive righteousness that bears fruit in a life of Christ-resembling righteousness, then others will hate you.

I should note that not every non-Christian hates genuine Christians. Not all worldly individuals and institutions are on a mission to wipe Christians off the face of the earth. In fact, many unbelievers see Christians and Christianity as a good thing, by and large, for society. So people *can* be attracted to how closely you conform to the likeness of Jesus, especially if they know that you were a real piece of work (like I was!) before salvation. Jesus will say as much a few verses later in the Sermon on the Mount: "In the same way, let your light shine before others, so that they may see your good works and give glory to your Father who is in heaven" (Matthew 5:16). Doing just that, the early church enjoyed great favor with people (Acts 2:47). A Christ-centered righteous life has a certain winsomeness about it.

At the same time, the book of Acts also tells us that because of the gospel "there arose . . . a great persecution against the church in Jerusalem, and they were all scattered throughout the regions of Judea and Samaria" (Acts 8:1). Some towns found Christianity interesting and socially beneficial while others tried to beat it to a pulp. You would not think that being a better person would make people dislike you. If you become more loving, more patient, more kind, more humble, more tactful, less jealous, less arrogant, less provoked, less willing to hold a grudge—if you become more like Jesus—you might expect people to like you *more*, not less, and certainly not to hate you, mock you, or even want to kill you. But the fact is that even as Christianity seems profoundly attractive to the human heart, it also offends deeply. Just look at what the comprehensively perfect Jesus endured, and you will see that people in their natural condition just cannot stomach righteousness.

Two Kinds of Stomachs: Relativists and Moralists

We will consider two different kinds of people who find the righteousness of Jesus offensive. On the one hand are relativists—people who believe that morality is relative or at least personal. On the other hand are religious moralists—people who believe that their high moral achievements should earn the attention of others, including

God. These perspectives motivate particular kinds of persecution against righteousness.

Relativists live according to their preferences, believing that they should do what they feel like doing and that no one else has the right to say they should do anything different. They find Christians annoying because their attitudes, words, and behaviors effectively condemn relativists for theirs. Christians submit themselves to Jesus as Lord, deferring to the gospel as their rule of life, but relativists obey their own sensibilities, so they tend to think of Christians as imposing high and unnecessary or arbitrary ethical standards upon themselves and others. This can make relativists overly sensitive around Christians. For example, I cannot tell you how many people have apologized to me for using profanity. If they spent some time with me and knew that I was a Christian (even before I was a pastor), they apparently concluded that I would find their language and joking inappropriate. Many Christians have had the same experience: being around someone who is growing in Christlikeness engenders a reforming impulse even in irreligious people.

Of course, apology is not persecution, but the same felt offense often leads to verbal persecution. The word translated "revile" in Matthew 5:11 means to heap insults or disparaging and unjustified words on someone. Jesus says that Christians can expect to feel the sting of slander—people falsely saying all kinds of evil against us because of our relationship with him. You may find yourself as the object of scorn and mocking: "Oh, you better not say that around Mary. She's a Christian." Or you may find guys deliberately sharing porn with you on the job site or repeatedly inviting you to a strip club with a look of disgust as you again say no. You may find your relatives standing up and yelling at you at a wedding or a funeral or a bridal shower. You may find people from your own family taking your pictures down from their walls or even disowning you. You may find your coworkers incensed that as a result of coming to know Jesus, you have begun to report all of your income to the IRS.

However the persecution comes, relativists usually take their shots from a deep sense that what you are doing is right whereas what they are doing is wrong. Your very existence will rub them the wrong way because it implicitly condemns their whole way of life as displeasing to God. "Stop judging me," they will say, even if you never once said a condemnatory word. Jesus has helpfully diagnosed their condition: "The light has come into the world, and people loved the darkness rather than the light because their works were evil. For everyone who does wicked things hates the light and does not come to the light, lest his works should be exposed" (John 3:19–20). Your light shines in their darkness, so they squint and put their hands over their faces and pull the covers up over their heads: they persecute you simply because they want the light turned off. Your light exposes them for who they are, and they do not want to go there. They hate you because your growth in Christ's righteousness brings into sharp relief their lack of righteousness.

The religious person, on the other hand, hates you and your righteousness not so much because of your increasing Christlikeness but because you have the audacity to claim that your righteousness is not your own. The fact that you have not worked up or earned or patched together some measure of righteousness that God finds acceptable enrages religious moralists. They will say, "All you do is cry out to God for his righteousness as a gift, and that somehow makes you perfectly acceptable to God? No matter what you have done? Then what is the point of being good?" Similarly, if the wicked prosper, religious people despair with the psalmist: "All in vain have I kept my heart clean and washed my hands in innocence" (Psalm 73:13).

When religious moralists hear that your acceptance with God is not at all based on your performance and that *every* performance falls flat—not only insufficient to God but actually detestable before him—they will become even more irate. They will not just think that what you say is nonsense; they will be livid because it implies that the project they have pursued all their lives (doing better, doing more) amounts to nothing but a pile of garbage. This is why the religious leaders wanted Jesus dead and mocked him and spit on him and had him beaten and crucified: he had the audacity to suggest that the sum total of their lives was nothing more than a crass attempt to manipulate God into giving them what they wanted, into obligating God (who owes us nothing) to accept them.

So we see that both religious moralists and relativists have plenty of reason to hate Christians, and the reason is righteousness—the perfect record achieved by Jesus Christ himself, which he gives to everyone who hungers and thirsts for it as a gift. What makes Christians so distasteful to non-Christians, religious or otherwise, is God's grace at the center of their lives.[79] Relativists find Christians annoyingly happy to obey God, and religious people find Christians annoyingly deprecating about their own moral accomplishments. Meanwhile, those persecuted for the sake of righteousness—for the sake of Jesus—are truly blessed. After all, they enjoy good company: they have real camaraderie with the prophets who came before, blessed also to belong to the kingdom of heaven and to have a heavenly reward.

The Blessing of a Kingdom and a Reward

What makes the persecuted so blessed? Jesus does not actually say that their righteousness makes them blessed; instead, Jesus says their persecution means two things are true for them, and those two things are the reason for their blessedness. First, the persecuted are blessed because they belong to the kingdom of heaven: their persecution reveals their citizenship. Second, the persecuted are blessed because they will receive a heavenly reward: they look forward to something far better.

The Blessing of a Kingdom. Belonging to God's kingdom is a blessing in itself, permanently joining the Christian to an everlasting kingdom, but it also entails living under God's rule now, and that yields persecution. Living your life under the Jesus Administration means that in this life you carry a cross just like your king did: heaven's king wore a crown of thorns before he wore a crown of gold (Revelation 14:14). If the world hated Jesus, it will hate his servants also (John 15:18–20). We are no better than our master.

So belonging to God's kingdom *now* means we live in a place of paradox—we belong, and while we wait to see the kingdom come to its fruition, we suffer. Bearing insults for the name of Jesus means that you are genuinely a part of his kingdom: "If you are insulted for the name of Christ, you are blessed, because the Spirit of glory and of God rests upon you" (1 Peter 4:14). This should not trouble you but should instead encourage you. D. A. Carson put it like this: "Far from being a depressing prospect, their suffering under persecution . . . becomes a triumphant sign that the kingdom is theirs."[80] It certainly seems like a dreadful thing to suffer persecution for the sake of righteousness, but you should find great consolation and true blessedness in the fact that your experience of persecution means that you have certainly been rescued from the domain of darkness and transferred to the kingdom of God's beloved Son (Colossians 1:13).

The Blessing of a Reward. In this verse, Jesus gives us incentive to endure persecution joyfully rather than with gritted teeth. And that incentive is God himself. Note that Jesus does not say, "Great is your reward in the most boring and dreadful place in the universe" but "Great is your reward in heaven," and since we know (see chapter 2) that the Jews of Jesus' day would have understood the word "heaven" as a circumlocution for "God," we can read this statement as saying that the persecuted are blessed because they have a great reward with God. This does not exclude the idea of heaven as the place where Christians go to be with God at the end of their lives (or the end of this age): that will be the time and place where God metes out our reward. But the focus here is on God himself, not the place where he may be, and on the rewards that he gladly gives to his children.

Rewards? You may have done a double take at that word. Indeed, God accepts you based on sheer grace, not your record or merits or achievements or theological background. Grace means that God welcomes you where you don't belong, "let into a place where you don't have the right to be."[81] Your nose is pressed to the glass, you long to be accepted, given a seat at that table, invited to that party . . . because you know this is what you were made for, yet you also know deep down that you have no right to be there. What you deserve for your sin is God's rejection. But instead of giving you what you deserve, he gives Jesus what you deserve, gives you what Jesus deserved, and accepts you on Jesus' record. As soon as you acknowledge before God that your sin and self-righteousness have stripped you of any right to fellowship with him, the doors of acceptance open wide, and you are welcomed into the place you have no right to be. That is grace.

And that may seem like "reward" enough, but Jesus says that the persecuted should expect a great reward in heaven. The word here is *not* used "in the sense of an earned payment . . . but of a freely given recompense, out of all proportion to the service."[82] God chooses to give the persecuted a gift for their suffering, and the gift will be way out of proportion to what they suffered. Paul puts it this way: "For this light momentary affliction is preparing for us an eternal weight of glory beyond all comparison" (2 Corinthians 4:17). A reward is not a wage: our king does not owe you anything, but because he is generous, he wants to reward you. Think of a father giving his child a monetary reward for mowing the lawn or cleaning out the garage. He has every right to require his son to do these chores as matters of duty and is not obligated to pay him a dime, but a generous father may want to incentivize the duty by promising a reward. It is a gift because it is gratuitous—unearned, uncalled for, having no return benefit for the giver. But it is a reward because the giver means it as incentive for service. You would have had to do it anyway, but the father, as an expression of his generosity, wants to encourage your obedience with the promise of a reward, or a gift-incentive.

What if you then yield to persecution because you know about the promised reward? It may seem wrong or disingenuous to serve Jesus in suffering for the reward. You should do it just for its own sake, right? Surely your obedience (whatever form that takes) should be motivated only by gratitude for what Jesus has done for you on the cross and gratitude for his giving you his perfect record as a gift. But Jesus has absolutely no problem motivating obedience with the promise of reward. Not only here in Matthew 5:12 but *many* times throughout Matthew's gospel, Jesus motivates service exactly the same way (see 5:46, 6:1, 6:2–4, 6:5–6, 6:16–18, 10:41–42). If Jesus himself holds out the promise of reward for us to consider, then it must be legitimate motivation.

Why, then, does the idea of serving the Lord for the reward rub most of us the wrong way? We often think that it invalidates or cancels out the motivation of gratitude, but does it really? Not if we have the same gratitude for the reward as we do for what Jesus has already done for us. After all, the thing that makes the reward possible is exactly the same thing that made Jesus' work on your behalf possible in the first place—the grace of God. When you understand that a reward is not a wage, you will not receive your reward at the final judgment and then throw a party for yourself. You will not pat yourself on the back for a job well done. Instead, you will worship Jesus alone as worthy of glory, just like we see in Revelation 4:10–11.

Perhaps, then, the main reason why the idea of serving Jesus for the reward sounds so horrible to us is that we do not understand what the reward is. Think about how the Bible describes heavenly reward—depicted with symbolic objects like crowns, the reward we will receive is ever-widening, ever-deepening, ever-increasing joy in knowing the Lord, for "this is eternal life, that they know you the only true God, and Jesus Christ whom you have sent" (John 17:3). Who doesn't want that? It *would* be wrong to incentivize your obedience to the Lord with the promise of cars and houses and health and wealth and prosperity and notoriety. That would make Christianity mercenary. But knowing Jesus more, seeing Jesus more, loving Jesus more, worshiping Jesus more, being like Jesus more, serving Jesus more, enjoying Jesus and all his benefits for all eternity more and more and more—*Jesus* is the reward promised to the persecuted. And if he is the reward, then it just makes sense to incentivize our persecution *for* Jesus with the reward *of* Jesus.

Is Jesus your idea of great reward? Think about if you got married for the reward of loving the one you love more deeply—that is actually the best possible motive in the world, because marriage is not about money but love. The same thing is true for the Christian faith. You join a new kingdom and then enjoy living in it, no matter what that living looks like. Christianity is about knowing the one true God and Jesus Christ whom he has sent—both now and with greater depth in the future. So your persecution for righteousness is blessed because it marks you as a citizen of the kingdom, but also because it yields you a great heavenly reward.

The First Commandment (in the Sermon on the Mount)

On the basis of citizenship and sure reward, Jesus finally gives the first command in the Sermon on the Mount. So far, we have only seen "blessings, not requirements,"[83] but Jesus tells us to do something at the beginning of verse 12: "Rejoice and be glad!" Because we are citizens of the kingdom, because we are in good company with the persecuted prophets, because we await a heavenly reward, we ought to rejoice. Indeed, we *must* rejoice and be glad. This is one of the most amazing features of the Christian life: amid the deepest possible pain, we can rejoice and literally jump for joy because our lives are not rooted or determined by the changing winds of circumstance but by a glorious relationship with Jesus that can never change.

Too often, we face trial like practical atheists, as though we are alone in the universe without a heavenly Father who cares for us. We hit back or pout or act like we do not care, or we might (out of a sense of piety) even pretend to enjoy it.[84] Jesus would never tell us to enjoy pain, but he would also never tell us to bury our heads in the sand. Instead, he commands us to analyze the harsh reality of life in a fallen world through the lens of God's grace. When you understand the gospel and know what is yours in Christ, you will say when persecuted, "What a privilege to suffer shame for Jesus' name. He suffered so much for me! What a blessing to suffer a little bit for him." Today's pain is still pain, but it is nothing compared with eternal glory.

Christians acknowledge the harsh reality of life in this age and the glorious reality of life in the age to come: "Christianity is not finally about anesthetizing us to life's pain, or even about waking us up to it and teaching us to live with it. It is about teaching us to live with a transforming longing, with a growing faith, with a sure and certain hope of what's to come."[85] Rejoice, therefore, and be glad because you are citizens of the kingdom of heaven along with all those who suffered before you. You do not have what it takes and your own moral excellence falls far short of the goal, yet you have waiting for you in heaven an eternal reward that will more than make up for all your suffering for Jesus. It will be Jesus himself, so delight yourself in him.

FOR YOUR HEAD

1. What difference does it make that the heavenly reward is a gift rather than a wage?
2. Why is persecution an essential component of kingdom life?

FOR YOUR HEART

3. When we read the Bible's teaching about Christian suffering, we can often feel afraid. Describe a time when you experienced that kind of fear and how this beatitude speaks to it.
4. Discuss a time when you suffered "persecution" for being foolish. Discuss another time when you suffered real persecution for being faithful. What was the difference? How did you respond to each kind of persecution?

FOR YOUR CHURCH

5. Identify someone in your Christian community who is currently being persecuted for righteousness' sake. What does this beatitude suggest about how you should minister to that person?
6. Brainstorm ways to prepare your church for persecution. If you do not face it now, how can you get ready for it when it comes?

FOR YOUR CITY

7. Tim Keller has said, "If we get through our lives as Christians without upsetting or offending anyone, we have not ministered with integrity."[86] Discuss your failures to communicate the gospel boldly for fear of persecution. Take a moment to pray for boldness.
8. Now discuss your successes preaching the gospel in the face of opposition—when you were bold without being belligerent. Take a moment to thank God for your boldness.

10

JESUS IS THE BEATITUDES

Presents are made for the pleasure of who gives them, not
the merits of who receives them.

> The father in Carlos Ruiz Zafón's
> *The Shadow of the Wind*

He opened his mouth . . . And when Jesus finished
these sayings, the crowds were astonished at his
teachings.

> – Matthew 5:2, 7:28

began this book by lamenting how dangerous it is to teach the
Beatitudes as a rulebook for better living. This kind of teaching
is alarmingly common, training us in an insipid brand of works-
righteousness. Now that we have seen how the Beatitudes reveal the
gospel, do you agree with me about the perils of presenting these
verses as mere moral lessons or goals for civil behavior? Indeed, have
I disabused you of the use of flannelgraph to teach the Beatitudes? I
certainly hope so. These verses convey the essence of the gospel, but
when reduced to flat moralistic teaching, they lose all their richness.

In fact, that kind of teaching is just wrong. The Beatitudes are far too radical to be reduced to felt figures or construction paper.

Let me be clear: I don't want to encourage some kind of new moralism where we think we have gotten too smart for simple stories presented beautifully. We never grow out of the gospel, and in many ways, the gospel is the simplest story ever. The Bible has also inspired tremendous art throughout the ages, and those creative expressions are certainly not a waste of time. Art, whether designed for concrete minds or abstract ones, has its purpose in God's world. God has designed his Scripture so that the most bookish and the most simple among us—even children—can understand his truth and worship him for who he is.

So this book is not about what children's Sunday school curriculum should or should not look like. In fact, we could all learn something from good teaching for children—namely, that we should never mature out of childlike awe. I have heard new believers ask good questions about key ideas in the Bible only to get complex jargon-laden answers from mature saints. Why do we not first give straightforward answers in language anyone can understand? It's no wonder that some unbelievers think Christians are stuck-up insiders.

No, I do not aim with this book to abolish all flannelgraph from every Sunday school classroom in the world. Flannelgraph has its place. I just want you to think before you use it as to whether it suits the Scripture you are teaching. We in the church do great harm when we claim that some passage of Scripture teaches something that it does not teach, especially when we boil that Scripture down to some neat moral lesson that requires more pulling up by the bootstraps than grasping at grace. Generations of young Christians can grow up with a false sense of piety. Mature adults will flee the church because it seems like an ineffective self-help club. But more importantly, God himself will be misrepresented, and his glory sullied, when those who claim to be his children act like his gospel is little more than a leg up in life.

When it comes to the Beatitudes, we simply need to read them as they are, not as our idol-factory hearts will remake them. Our flesh desperately wants to rewrite the Beatitudes as reductionist epigrams when Jesus is preaching nothing less or more than the gospel! The Sermon on the Mount is no rulebook for better living but the exposition of life-giving grace. The Beatitudes specifically assume that "blessed" people have come to the end of themselves. They realize that their own moral excellence won't cut it. They can hardly believe that Jesus crucified morality as they know it when he died on the cross for their sins—for all the bad and all the good they ever did. And they rejoice at the grace that makes them so blessed.

So take a few steps back and marvel. The Beatitudes reveal the profile of the Christian, the character of the one who has had a life-changing encounter with the grace of God. In light of God's overwhelming goodness, the sinner sees his own poverty of spirit and mourns not only for his own sin but also for the spiritual sickness of the world. Therefore, he grows meek and longs all the more earnestly for true righteousness. Therefore, he practices mercy and enjoys purity and makes peace. Therefore, he gladly endures persecution for the sake of Jesus.

No one could earn this kind of spiritual résumé on his own, no matter how hard he tried. Except for Jesus.

Jesus and the Beatitudes

Apart from grace, the Beatitudes set an impossible standard. We may look at them and think, "Well, Jesus, thanks for letting me in on the fact that I'll never be blessed. Guess I'll just plug along with the rest of my useless life now." But you *can* embody the Beatitudes through grace—because Jesus Christ lived them for you and died so that you could enjoy true blessing in him. That's actually what makes the Beatitudes so radical. It's not *what they say* so much as the person to whom they refer: they are all about Jesus Christ.

In chapter 1, I mentioned some references from Matthew's gospel that show how Jesus fulfills the Beatitudes. Let's now look more carefully at Jesus as Matthew reveals him. We will quickly see that he must be the most blessed person ever.

How poor in spirit was Jesus? Astonishingly, the King of kings humbled himself to the lowest possible point in order to redeem you.

During the incarnation, Jesus never assumed his own authority but always deferred to his heavenly Father and to the scripture. In Matthew 4:1–11, the devil tempted Jesus to assert himself and show his greatness, but he refused three times over. Why? "The Son of Man came not to be served but to serve" (20:28). As Paul would write later, "he was in the form of God, did not count equality with God a thing to be grasped, but made himself nothing" (Philippians 2:6–7). Jesus was completely "lowly in heart" (Matthew 11:29). You think you are something? Jesus was everything, yet he chose to be a servant.

Did Jesus mourn? Yes, but not his own sin, for he had none. Instead, he mourned the sin of the world—that which afflicts us all. It might seem more reasonable that Jesus would respond to our sin with indignation, for all sin is an unjust affront to God in his holiness, and it cost Jesus his life even though he never contributed one ounce to it. Yes, he had harsh words for those who refused to repent despite seeing his great works (Matthew 11:20–24), but even those words revealed a heart of great mourning: sin saddened Jesus, and he had compassion on those who suffered because of it (see 9:6; 14:14; 15:32). That's why Jesus spent his last hours in sorrow, for he then began to see the full extent of what he would have to endure if he would redeem us from our sin (see 26:37–39). Jesus mourned your sin more deeply than you ever have.

Was Jesus meek? Consider the temptation of Jesus in Matthew 4 again: the devil invited him to display his power extravagantly, but Jesus had great self-control to keep his power in check until the time that his Father chose to reveal it. Even when he was transfigured to shine as brightly as the sun, Jesus spoke gently with his terrified disciples and instructed them to tell no one what had happened until after his resurrection (17:1–13). Later, he entered Jerusalem "triumphantly" on a pathetic donkey, not a stallion (21:1–11). Jesus did not need or want fanfare, even if it seemed completely justified. He confronted and offended where appropriate, but only for the sake of righteousness. He never thought he was too good for anyone, so he paid his taxes (17:27; 22:21) and rebuked his disciples when they thought he had better things to do than pray with children (see

18:13–15). What do you think you deserve? Jesus never demanded any praise for himself even though he deserves it all.

Did Jesus hunger and thirst for righteousness? Yes and no. Jesus did not long for righteousness in the same way that we do . . . because he lived a perfectly righteous life. Even unbelievers like Pilate's wife could recognize that (Matthew 27:19). But he could not have done anything less. He revealed his nearness to his Father in the most intense moments of his life, as he awaited arrest and as he hung on the cross—he drew near to his Father with complete confidence then, and he did so with confidence because he lived a life completely beyond reproach. Jesus never did anything that failed in any respect before God, who found him utterly acceptable and pleasing (17:5). Can you meet this standard? Not on your own. But praise God that Jesus meets it for you!

Was Jesus merciful? Time and again, Jesus revealed his willingness to heal people from various afflictions (Matthew 4:23–24). He healed a leper (8:1–4) and a servant (8:5–13) and a mother-in-law (8:14) and a paralytic (9:2–8) and a dead daughter (9:18–25) and blind men (9:27–30; 20:29–34) and someone with a withered hand (12:10–13) and those sick with all kinds of disease (14:35–36). He cast out demons (8:16, 28–32; 9:32–33; 15:22–28) and calmed a storm to calm his disciples' worries (8:23–27) and fed thousands of hungry people (14:13–21; 15:32–38). Besides doing mercy, he taught mercy as well, for he knew that his Father would pursue every lost sheep to the very end (18:10–14). His was a ministry of mercy, and he equipped his disciples for the same (10:1).

But Jesus' mercy penetrated deeper than our physical misery; it moved into the deepest recesses of our hearts by forgiving us of the sin that drives *all* our misery. He forgave the paralytic even before he healed his paralysis (Matthew 9:2). And he depicted the Father's forgiveness vividly in the parable of the unforgiving servant, showing his lavish, debt-canceling love (18:21–35). Jesus had extravagant mercy for the unmerciful—that is, sinners like you and me. It is not because of your mercy that you will receive mercy. No, Jesus' mercy is a gift you receive by faith.

Did Jesus have a pure heart? Jesus had no conflict within him, gladly and single-heartedly devoted to doing only and always exactly what his Father wanted him to do. He willingly and completely submitted himself to his Father even when faced with the worst possible death as he would drink God's cup of wrath against all sin: "Not as I will, but as you will," he said (Matthew 26:39). Purity of heart does not mean that he went to the cross blasé about its painful reality, but he was fixed on that end because his mind was resolutely set on the things of God (16:21–23). Our Savior was simultaneously realistic about the world and utterly single-minded about heavenly things. Christ alone achieved purity of heart.

Was Jesus a peacemaker? Jesus sometimes rustled feathers, and he called out sin where he saw it (even sometimes making a mess in the process, like when he cleansed the temple in Matthew 21:12–13), but he could also bring surprising kinds of peace to tense situations. Consider the Pharisees trying to make him seem like a political rebel: Jesus shut them up with a submissive response that made them marvel (Matthew 22:15–22). Right after that, the Sadducees had a similar plan to test Jesus, but his answer astonished the crowds (22:23–33). Even people who tried their hardest to corner Jesus found him even-keeled, and Jesus made peace with his words in those situations. But he did his final act of peacemaking on the cross, reconciling sinners to God so that they could access him in his holiness freely and openly (27:51). Jesus made peace with God for rebels who did not even know they were at war with God—ignorant rebels like you and me.

Did Jesus suffer persecution for righteousness' sake? In Isaiah 53, the prophet said Jesus would be hated, bullied, and full of sorrow. We see the full picture of that in the Gospels, for no one was ever persecuted like Jesus. Even his close friends did not really understand him, and his enemies frequently spent their creative energies trying to come up with traps for him. In the end, they seemed to win because Jesus was condemned for evil he never committed, mocked, whipped, beaten nearly to the point of death, and then crucified (Matthew 27:26–50). But Jesus never sinned, having lived a completely righteous life, and his Father vindicated him for that by raising him from the dead (28:6). Jesus was raised from the dead so that you can enjoy newness of life (see Romans 6:4).

Even if we consider Matthew's gospel alone, we see sufficient evidence that Jesus himself fulfills the Beatitudes. Indeed, the Beatitudes are all about Jesus. They are all about what it means to bear God's image in the world. No path to special spiritual achievement, they simply profile the one who knows God and his grace. And the good news for sinners like us is that Jesus does not speak the Beatitudes to condemn us but to free us. He fulfills them, so we rejoice and seek him, and *then* the Beatitudes become true of us as well.

Get Clear on the Gospel

Jesus taught with a kind of authority that the people in his day had never heard (Matthew 7:28–29) because he taught what he lived: the gospel of God. Consider the context of the Sermon on the Mount and you will see that it is just an instance in which Jesus was "proclaiming the gospel of the kingdom" (Matthew 4:23), or explaining the good news of God's grace to man. Put another way, the Sermon on the Mount is the expression of a life gripped by God's grace. That's why it's the most relevant sermon ever preached. Every sinner—unbelieving *and* believing—needs the gospel.

The good news of the kingdom—of God's gracious rule over redeemed sinners—should make every heart glad. Can you imagine any kind of "blessedness" that does not include redemption from sin? And God's kingdom hardly concerns itself with anything else. In God's kingdom, the servants have their debt settled by the unobligated and gracious king (Matthew 18:27). In God's kingdom, the workers get more than they earned (Matthew 20:9). My sin is so great that I qualify only for rejection by God, but the good news is that I can receive mercy and grace from him through Jesus Christ.

But look more closely at what happens in those passages I just mentioned about what God's kingdom is like. In Matthew 18, a man suffers completely justified punishment for taking out more loans than he can repay, and his master has compassion on him and forgives the debt. In Matthew 20, some people work all day and others work

121

only the last part of the day, but they all receive a day's wages. Do these stories seem fair to you? The first one may seem kind, and you may want the same kind of treatment, but it isn't actually fair. The second one probably seems positively undemocratic. Does it rub you the wrong way when people do not get the punishment they seem to deserve? What about when people get more money or kindness than they seem to have earned?

Jesus told these stories because they show us the nature of God and his kingdom. If you don't like them, then you do not get the gospel. You and I are like that man who owed an enormous debt and was therefore justly enslaved as payment, yet who found himself forgiven by the very one to whom he owed the debt. You and I are like the laborer who came in just at the end of the day, yet received as much as if he had worked all day, because the grace of the kingdom reflects the generosity of the king, not the work of the servants. Jesus and his atoning work on the cross has no rival when it comes to good news because sinners enter his kingdom only through him and his righteousness, and that is the best news I could ever hear. Jesus came to live the life I should have lived and die the death I should have died. He does not, then, offer the Beatitudes as self-help advice. No, the Beatitudes simply express what a life profoundly changed by Jesus looks like.

We want to reduce the Beatitudes to a list of dos and don'ts for how to live life once you get the gospel figured out—as though once you have the baby-stuff gospel under your belt, you can move on to practical life and making yourself into a full-fledged Christian. Those transformed by God's grace do live profoundly differently than they did when they were under the condemnation of sin, but not because they follow certain requirements about how to be Christian; rather, they have encountered God's grace and are completely changed from the inside out. They pursue moral lives, but not because they think their own moral excellence earns them favor with God; they know that grace alone makes them acceptable before God and that Jesus died to free them from their own moralism. So the Beatitudes describe what happens "naturally" through the Spirit in a life ruled by

God's grace. Moralism is irrelevant and hypocrisy is exposed: only grace remains.

No one can "do" the Beatitudes. You either have that profile as a gift of grace or not. But oh how beautiful they are! When you get the gospel, you enjoy the blessedness of living in the center of the most radical kingdom ever conceived. You know without a doubt that you did not get into that kingdom by your own moral efforts; quite the contrary, Jesus died so that your own spiritual résumé could go onto the dung heap where it belongs. If your life bears any resemblance to the Beatitudes, it is because you are blessed in Jesus—you died with him so that you might live in him. The Beatitudes flesh out outrageous grace, which is yours as a gift through the gospel.

FOR YOUR HEAD

1. What is so dangerous about reducing the Beatitudes to a list of dos and don'ts?
2. How does Jesus fulfill each of the Beatitudes?

FOR YOUR HEART

3. Some of us are more prone to moralism than others, so how do you see yourself leaning toward that as you study the Beatitudes? In what ways do you find yourself wanting to make a clear list of behaviors that fit and don't fit the kingdom so that you can live accordingly and earn God's favor? At what point or points in the Beatitudes are you tempted to make rules for yourself and/or for others?
4. You may be tempted now to focus outward and judge others for their rule-making, using your new or renewed light on the Beatitudes to hammer others for how poorly they have understood or taught these verses. What do the Beatitudes themselves have to say about such an attitude?
5. Take some time in personal prayer to worship Jesus for how perfectly he fulfills the Beatitudes. Read back through the gospel according to Matthew and look for how Jesus reveals himself as the most blessed person alive.

FOR YOUR CHURCH

6. How might understanding that the Beatitudes describe Jesus perfectly affect how you do church? For example, discuss how Jesus' poverty of spirit might affect your church's approach to personal discipleship.

FOR YOUR CITY

7. How clear are you about the gospel? Does that word "gospel" strike you as mysterious or difficult to define? Can you only use "church" words to define it? How might you grow both in your understanding of the gospel and in your ability to communicate it to others both inside and outside the church community?

8. How might understanding that the Beatitudes describe the profile of a Christian affect how you "love your neighbor" through community ministry? For example, discuss how your personal poverty of spirit might affect your involvement in local affairs.

NOTES

1. D. Martyn Lloyd-Jones, *Studies in the Sermon on the Mount* (Grand Rapids, MI: Eerdmans, 1984), 24.

2. D. A. Carson, *Jesus' Sermon on the Mount and His Confrontation with the World: An Exposition of Matthew 5–10* (Grand Rapids, MI: Baker, 1987), 16–17.

3. John MacArthur, *The MacArthur New Testament Commentary: Matthew 1–7* (Chicago: Moody Bible Institute, 1985), 142

4. Edward T. Welch, *Shame Interrupted: How God Lifts the Pain of Worthlessness and Rejection* (Greensboro, NC: New Growth, 2012), 141.

5. Phillip Yancey, *The Jesus I Never Knew* (Grand Rapids, MI: Zondervan, 2002), 113. Eugene Peterson also used the word "lucky" to describe blessedness in his poem series "Holy Luck," originally published in *Theology Today* 44 (April 1987): 95–102.

6. N. T. Wright, "Heaven Is Not Our Home," *Christianity Today*, April 2008, http://www.christianitytoday.com/ct/2008/april/13.36.html (emphasis added).

7. Carson, *Jesus' Sermon*, 12.

8. Paul David Tripp, *A Quest for More: Living for Something Bigger Than You* (Greensboro, NC: New Growth, 2007), 66–68.

9. John Calvin, *Golden Booklet of the True Christian Life* (Grand Rapids, MI: Baker, 1952), 32.

10. Carson, *Jesus' Sermon*, 18.

11. Robert H. Mounce, *Matthew* (Peabody, MA: Hendrickson, 1991), 38.

12. Thomas Watson, *The Beatitudes: An Exposition of Matthew 5:1–12* (1660; Banner of Truth, 1985), 45.

13. Lloyd-Jones, *Studies*, 35.

14. Carson, *Jesus' Sermon*, 18 (emphasis added).

15. Lloyd-Jones, *Studies*, 34.

16. Carson, *Jesus' Sermon*, 19.

17. Watson, *Beatitudes*, 87.

18. Mounce, *Matthew*, 39.

19. Watson, *Beatitudes*, 61.

20. Timothy Keller and J. Allen Thompson, *Church Planter Manual* (New York: Redeemer Presbyterian Church, 2002), 190.

21. Bob Kauflin revised original lyrics by John Newton for the contemporary hymn "The Look" available on the album "Upward: The Bob Kauflin Hymns Project" (Sovereign Grace Praise, 2003).

22. John R. W. Stott, *The Message of the Sermon on the Mount: Christian Counter-Culture* (Westmont, IL: InterVarsity, 1978), 42.

23. Carson, *Jesus' Sermon*, 20.

24. See Lloyd-Jones, *Studies*, 56.

25. See D. A. Carson, *Matthew: Chapters 1–12*, The Expositor's Bible Commentary (Grand Rapids, MI: Zondervan, 1995), 20, and Lloyd-Jones, *Studies*, 54ff.

26. Watson, *Beatitudes*, 106.

27. "To be truly meek means we no longer protect ourselves, because we see there is nothing worth defending" (Lloyd-Jones, *Studies*, 57).

28. Carson, *Matthew*, 133.

29. Robert A. Smith, *Matthew*, Augsburg Commentary on the New Testament (Minneapolis: Augsburg Fortress, 1989), 83.

30. Lloyd-Jones, *Studies*, 58.

31. Carson, *Jesus' Sermon*, 20.

32. Lloyd-Jones, *Studies*, 54.

33. W. D. Davies and D. C. Allison, *A Critical and Exegetical Commentary on the Gospel According to Saint Matthew, Volume 1: Introduction and Commentary on Matthew 1–7* (London: T&T Clark, 1988), 452.

34. Michael Green, *The Message of Matthew: The Kingdom of Heaven* (Downers Grove, IL: InterVarsity, 2000), 90.

35. Carson, *Jesus' Sermon*, 23.

36. Timothy Keller, "New Life in Christ – 1," Redeemer Presbyterian Church in New York City, February 18, 1990.

37. Ibid.

38. Lloyd-Jones, *Studies*, 65.

39. Rick James, my Campus Crusade for Christ director in the early 1990s, used this illustration to explain our unsatisfying search for righteousness outside of Christ.

40. Lloyd-Jones, *Studies*, 98.

41. Ibid., 66.

42. Howard Peskett and Vinoth Ramachandra, *The Message of Mission: The Glory of Christ in All Time and Space* (Grand Rapids, MI: InterVarsity, 2003), 113–114.

43. Lloyd-Jones, *Studies*, 84.

44. See Psalm 103:8 and Genesis 19:16 respectively.

45. Davies and Allison, *Matthew*, 455.

46. Guelich, *Sermon on the Mount*, 104.

47. Carson, *Matthew*, 134.

48. Keller, "New Life in Christ – 1."

49. Mounce, *Matthew*, 40.

50. C. S. Lewis, *The Four Loves* (San Diego: Harvest, 1988), 120.

51. Timothy Keller, *The Reason for God* (New York: Dutton, 2008), 187–193.

52. Philip Yancey, *What's So Amazing About Grace?* (Grand Rapids, MI: Zondervan, 1995), 112.

53. Ibid., 96.

54. R. C. Sproul, *The Holiness of God* (Wheaton, IL: Tyndale, 1998), 111.

55. Timothy Keller, *Gospel in Life: Grace Changes Everything* (Grand Rapids, MI: Zondervan, 2010), 108.

56. Lloyd-Jones, *Studies*, 88.

57. Watson, *Beatitudes*, 175.

58. C. S. Lewis, *The Complete C. S. Lewis Signature Classics* (San Francisco: Harper, 2002), 113.

59. Davies and Allison, *Matthew*, 456.

60. Timothy Keller, "New Life in Christ – 2," Redeemer Presbyterian Church in New York City, February 25, 1990.

61. Green, *Matthew*, 91.

62. R. V. G. Tasker, *The Gospel According to St. Matthew: An Introduction and Commentary* (Grand Rapids, MI: Eerdmans, 1962), 62.

63. Guelich, *Sermon on the Mount*, 105.

64. Stott, *Message*, 49 (emphasis added).

65. Davies and Allison, *Matthew*, 456.

66. Stott, *Message*, 49.

67. Watson, *Beatitudes*, 182.

68. John Piper, "Blessed Are the Pure in Heart," March 2, 1986, http://www.desiringgod.org/resource-library/sermons/blessed-are-the-pure-in-heart.

69. Lloyd-Jones, *Studies*, 97.

70. Jonathan Edwards, *The Works of President Edwards* (New York: S. Converse, 1830), 8:526.

71. Guelich, *Sermon*, 106.

72. John Calvin, *Calvin's Commentaries*, Volume XVI (Grand Rapids, MI: Baker, 1996), 264.

73. Pink, *Beatitudes*, 53.

74. Lloyd-Jones, *Studies*, 104.

75. Guelich, *Sermon on the Mount*, 107.

76. Carson, *Jesus' Sermon*, 28.

77. Davies and Allison, *Matthew*, 459.

78. Lloyd-Jones, *Studies*, 112.

79. Watson, *Beatitudes*, 273.

80. Carson, *Jesus' Sermon*, 30.

81. Timothy Keller, "Faith Rising," Redeemer Presbyterian Church in New York City, August 12, 1990.

82. R. T. France, *Matthew*, The Tyndale New Testament Commentaries (Grand Rapids, MI: Eerdmans, 1985), 112.

83. Davies and Allison, *Matthew*, 466.

84. Stott, *Message*, 52.

85. Mark Dever, *The Gospel and Personal Evangelism* (Wheaton, IL: Crossway, 2007), 35.

86. Timothy Keller, *Evangelism: Studies in the Book of Acts* (New York: Redeemer Presbyterian Church, 2005), 212.